THREADS

*And we know that all things work together for good
to those who love God, to those who are the called
according to **His** purpose.*

*For whom He foreknew, He also predestined
to be conformed to the image of His Son,
that He might be the firstborn among many brethren.*

(Romans 8:28-29)

THREADS

A Revealing Journey Leading to Truth and Wholeness

TERI ANN MOYER

Carpenter's Son Publishing
COMMUNICATION BY DESIGN

Published by Carpenter's Son Publishing, Franklin, Tennessee and Communication by Design, Rancho Santa Margarita, California

Published in association with Larry Carpenter of Christian Book Services, LLC
www.christianbookservices.com

Unless otherwise noted, all Scripture quotations are taken from the New King James Version®. Copyright © 1982 by Thomas Nelson, Inc. Used by permission. All rights reserved.

Scripture quotations marked HCSB are taken from the Holman Christian Standard Bible®, Copyright © 1999, 2000, 2002, 2003, 2009 by Holman Bible Publishers. Used by permission. Holman Christian Standard Bible®, Holman CSB®, and HCSB® are federally registered trademarks of Holman Bible Publishers.

The names in this book have been changed out of respect for the privacy of the individuals mentioned.

Cover Design by Paul Lewis, LewisDM.com
Portrait photography by Vitaly Manzuk, vitalymanzuk.com
Cover photograph copyright © Dinamiracle/istockphoto.com (15089418)

Interior Design by Communication by Design
Interior images copyright © Shlapak Liliya/Shutterstock.com (93187291)
Interior image copyright © Swapan Photo./Shutterstock.com (82563967)
Interior image copyright © Theeradech Sanin/Shutterstock.com (134520248)
Interior image copyright © Zdenek Harnoch/Shutterstock.com (73722391)

Editing by Virginia Bowen and Lorraine Bossé-Smith
Proofread by Christa Schreckengost and Kari Windes

Printed in the United States of America
Downloadable lessons available at www.THREADSbyTeri.com

ISBN: 978-1-940262-27-7

18 17 16 15 14 13 12 11
10 9 8 7 6 5 4 3

In loving memory of Shawn Leslie,
my sister and my best friend.

As multitudes of thread colors are used to weave the most beautiful of tapestries, so the Lord uses a multitude of experiences to weave us into the people He created us to be.

CONTENTS

*Blessed **be** the God and Father of our Lord Jesus Christ,
who according to His abundant mercy has begotten us
again to a living hope through the resurrection of
Jesus Christ from the dead, to an inheritance
incorruptible and undefiled and that does not
fade away, reserved in heaven for you,
who are kept by the power of God through faith
for salvation ready to be revealed in the last time.*

*In this you greatly rejoice,
though now for a little while, if need be,
you have been grieved by various trials,
that the genuineness of your faith,
being much more precious than gold that perishes,
though it is tested by fire, may be found to praise,
honor, and glory at the revelation of Jesus Christ,
whom having not seen you love.*

*Though now you do not see **Him**, yet believing,
you rejoice with joy inexpressible and full of glory,
receiving the end of your faith—
the salvation of **your** souls.*

(1 Peter 1:3–9)

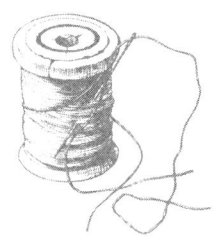

THANKS

First and foremost I thank Jesus Christ for leaving His throne to come to this earth for the sole purpose of taking the punishment due me upon Himself; without Him there would be no story. He is the weaver of this tapestry upon which He has chosen to place many a "thread." I thank the Lord for Lynda MacDonald, whom He used to show love beyond my comprehension, and for her husband, Pastor Byron MacDonald, whose teaching is biblically sound. I thank the Lord for my friend and sister in Christ, Gretchen Goldsmith, who continues to encourage me in and through the way she lives her life, the way she conducts business, and the way she raises her children. I thank the Lord for Rolling Hills Covenant Church[1] and the many Bible classes and ministries He allowed me to participate in there.

I thank the Lord for Greg Elsasser and Last Words Ministry[2] for being sensitive to the Holy Spirit and seeing something in me that I did not see myself, allowing me to serve alongside them in the production of *The Adventures of Roman and Jorge*[3]. I thank God for Cathe Laurie who has a wonderful heart for prayer; for her wisdom, love, and grace in leading the Harvest women's ministry, Virtue[4]. I thank the Lord for my pastor and teacher Greg Laurie who teaches straight from the Bible; for his calling and passion to preach the gospel. I thank the Lord for Harvest Orange County[5], for the love that is extended through the body of Christ, and for the many opportunities He has provided for me to serve there as I seek to glorify Him with my life.

I thank my mom who loves me the way she knows how and who continues to love me and grow in the grace and knowledge of the Lord. I thank my stepdad for nurturing the creative side God gave me and for stepping in when my biological father stepped out. I thank the Lord for my brothers and sisters in Christ, and the many others He is using to add color to this, yet unfinished, tapestry.

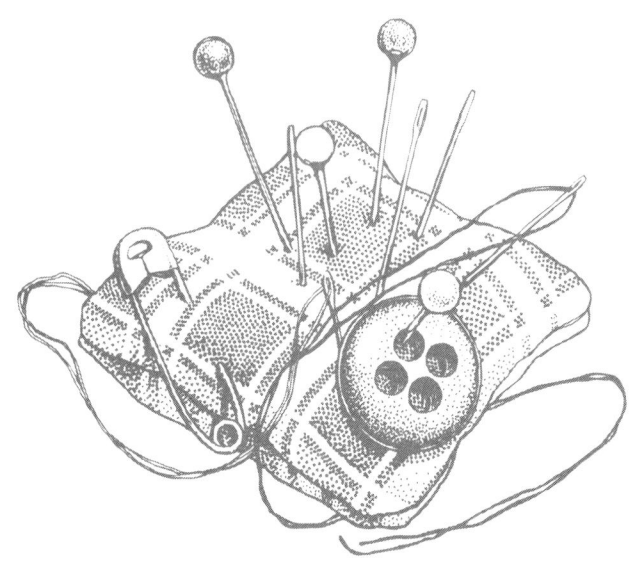

Now no chastening seems to be joyful for the present,
but painful; nevertheless, afterward it yields
the peaceable fruit of righteousness to those
who have been trained by it.

Therefore strengthen the hands
which hang down, and the feeble knees,
and make straight paths for your feet,
so that what is lame may not be dislocated,
but rather be healed.

(Hebrews 12:11–13)

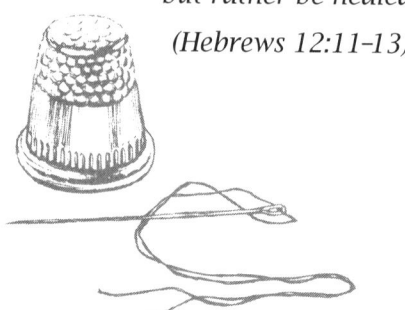

INTRODUCTION

I see life as an unfinished tapestry being woven by a mighty, loving God, who carefully chooses the colors of each individual thread, placing every single one exactly where it needs to go to weave us into the people He put us on this earth to be.

As multitudes of thread colors are used to weave the most beautiful of tapestries, so the Lord uses a multitude of experiences to weave us into the people He created us to be. Some experiences are wonderfully bright and cheerful; others are bleak, bland, and seem boring. The darkest times in our lives, the most difficult, are often the ones God dramatically uses for that punch of contrast. Then there's white, which brings out the highlights and opens our eyes to details otherwise unseen.

We may not like some of the colors God has chosen for our tapestry, but when it's fully complete, each color will make sense.

As Romans 8:28 states, "*All things work together for good to those who love God, to those who are called according to **His** purpose.*" We may not always have a clear picture of God's purpose for us in any given situation, especially in the dark and difficult times, but we can entrust our lives—our entire lives—to Him who knows exactly what He's doing and why.

So, upon these pages lies the evolution of a tapestry. Albeit incomplete, the hands of the One who is so masterfully weaving this tapestry can be seen in the threads chosen. My hope and prayer is the Lord might use these threads to inspire, encourage, and give you strength in the midst of darkness, to stand firm and remember God is weaving your life into something beautiful He will reveal on the day of completion (*James 1:2–4*).

A PRAYER FOR YOU

Father God, to each of us You have given a story—our lives—to do with what You will. Lord God, I pray the story You have allowed me to place upon these pages will touch the hearts of those who read it. Lord God, use each thread to reach those who read about the colors You have woven for them, in the way You choose to speak to them.

To bring them joy;
    to bring them peace;
        to bring them through sorrow and pain
        to the contentment only gained through
        trusting You completely with every part
        of their lives.

To teach them;
    to uphold them;
        to bring them wisdom;
            to impart to them grace;
                to show them the greatness
                of who You are;
                    to reveal to them Your mercy;
                        to reveal to them Your love.

Lord, be free to reach into the inner depths of every soul who reads this. You are the One who is creating this tapestry. You are the One who has so artistically woven each and every thread. To You be all glory, honor, and praise. In Jesus's gracious name I pray.

Amen.

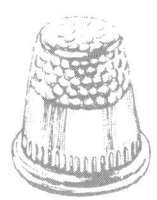

PINK

Ponytails, Sunday Dresses, 'n' Daddy

All dressed up and ready to go to church, eagerly awaiting her grandpa's arrival, a petite little girl sat poised and ready, her long blond hair pulled tightly back into a ponytail. Tina knew her grandpa would have a shiny, new silver dollar to give her; he always did.

She was four when he died. In sorrow, Tina took her two-year-old brother by the hand and ventured outside for a walk along the quiet suburban street. Looking up at the trees, leaves blowing in the wind, she imagined her grandpa in heaven.

"Look, Brent, I wonder if grandpa can see us from heaven." She exclaimed.

Tina's image of heaven was puffy white clouds, angels in white robes, and brilliant white light; like the beauty of the sun shining its rays through clouds after the rain, when the sky is crystal clear and God rains His sunshine down on earth. Just then, Tina's father came speeding around the corner in his red Corvair, pulled over, and yelled out the window, "What are you kids doing out here? Get home right now!"

Little Tina got in a lot of trouble that day. She spent the rest of the afternoon alone in her bedroom, laying face down on her bed sobbing, tears soaking the baby pink, ribbed cotton bedspread. Tina loved her grandpa; he was always so nice to her. He <u>saw</u> little Tina; not small and insignificant, but larger than life and creative, with an incessant imagination. Tina was sad when her grandpa died so hearing her father yell at her and send her to her room was devastating. To little Tina it seemed as though no one really cared her grandpa was gone, and she was a bad little girl for feeling sad. From this, Tina learned her feelings didn't matter; they were unimportant, and so was she. Little Tina felt broken.

Born and raised in sunny Southern California, Tina was the third of the four Miller children born to Bill and Martha Miller. The oldest of the four was her sister, Shawn; then came her two brothers, Todd (second to the oldest) and Brent (the youngest). The Miller family lived modestly in a three bedroom house. Like any other good, American, "Christian" family, the Miller's went to church on Sunday, prayed at dinner, and prayed again as the children were tucked into bed each night. Back then, to be American meant to be Christian, so they were.

The family stopped attending church services when the pastor they had grown to love left, but they continued praying those unforgettable prayers . . . "God is great, God is good, let us thank Him for our food," and "Now I lay me down to sleep . . ."

Tina believed in God and Jesus, and loved going to Sunday school at church, especially the arts and crafts projects. She doesn't recall learning much about God Himself, though. She knew Jesus was God's Son, that He was born of a virgin, and that's how Christmas came about. She also knew Jesus died on a cross and rose on the third day, and that's why Easter is celebrated.

As a young girl, little Tina wanted to be a nun, although she wasn't raised Catholic. She thought nuns were nice, more spiritual, and somehow closer to God. Besides, she liked the outfits they wore. Tina thought if she were to become a nun, she would know God better, and He might love her if she lived the solitary, good-girl life of a nun.

Tina was rather small for her age. As a matter of fact, when she was in first grade, one of the boys at school asked her if she was a midget. Kids can be so mean. She didn't see herself as small, and didn't understand why he would even ask her such a question. At the end of her first grade year, Tina's parents were advised it would be best to hold their daughter back a year, that perhaps she would catch up in size with the other girls her age. Tina didn't understand why she had to spend an extra year in first grade. Her older sister was small, too, but she wasn't put back a grade; so why little Tina? Her parents never told her why she was going back to first grade. Between the cruel comments from the other kids, and her own imagination, Tina came to the conclusion she was held back because she wasn't as smart as the other kids. Tina was extremely shy and insecure throughout her youth. When she was in junior high, she finally broke down and asked her mother. "Mom, did you really have me repeat first grade just because I was small, or was it because I wasn't as smart as the other kids?" Though her mother reassured Tina she was held back because of her small size, and it had nothing to do with her learning ability, Tina remained insecure.

Tina's mom and dad had a heated argument when he returned from one of his business trips and Bill stormed out the door. Her father didn't come home after that, except for a few short visits. Tina doesn't remember much about her biological father but she was told he was a smart man, with a genius-level IQ. She recalls her mother telling stories about her dad reading the encyclopedia cover-to-cover, and how he remembered every single word he read, proving it by sharing what he read with his friends and family. Bill was also a very creative man. With the predominance of pop art at the time, Bill made many large paintings similar in style to Andy Warhol. His uncle, Ray, was a multi-Oscar-winning set director, so creativity ran in the Miller family. Bill wasn't home much, and when he was, it wasn't for any length of time.

When Tina was five, she picked out some very special birthday presents for her father. She was out shopping with her mom, and they picked out two of his favorite things—Bing cherries, and a nice, white dress shirt. Tina couldn't wait for her daddy to come home so she could give him the birthday presents she picked out for him. She was so excited. When she heard him at the door, she ran to the front room. Her mom stood at the door and handed Tina's father the birthday presents. Tina's parents stood at the front door as an argument ensued. With little Tina standing in the background, her daddy threw the unwrapped birthday presents on the floor and stormed out the door. Tina never saw him again. Not only did Tina's daddy reject the birthday presents she picked out especially for him, he rejected her. "What did I do wrong?" Tina wondered. This was just one more thing to reinforce her feeling unworthy of love. If her own father rejected her, how could anyone accept her, or ever want to be her friend? Tina carried the notion that she was ugly, stupid, and totally unlovable for years.

Tina's parents divorced when she was six. Her dad moved to Florida, remarried, and had a son with his new wife. Tina doesn't recall her mom ever telling her that her daddy was never coming back, or even saying anything about a divorce. Bill just walked out the door, and Tina never saw or heard from him again. With no explanations as to Tina's dad's disappearance, she was, once again, left to her own imagination. In her little, six-year-old mind, she concluded she must have done something terribly wrong; she was bad, unwanted, and unlovable. She thought her daddy left because of her and, therefore, there must not be one single good thing about her; if her own father couldn't love her, how could anyone else ever love her?

One of Bill's best friends in high school, Larry, helped the Miller family a lot after Bill left. The Miller kids were without a father, and Larry's kids were without a mother, so the two families spent a lot of time together. When Tina was two years old, Larry's parents sold their house and bought a 40-foot sailboat they named *The Yankee*, which was fitting for the white beauty with her wood railings, blue trim, and red accents. Larry's parents moved out of their huge Palos Verdes home and onto *The Yankee*. The Miller family went to the boat a lot. Tina and her brothers and sister had a lot of fun hanging out with Larry's kids, swimming, sailing, painting, and making crafts with Larry's mother, Ruth, who was very creative and loved kids. Tina spent many an hour sitting on Ruth's soft, round lap while she read Tina stories using a host of character voices.

Martha and Larry got married when Tina was seven. Although they didn't get married in a church, the wedding seemed like a fairy tale to Tina. Tree-lined walkways led to a small, storybook building covered with lush, green ivy. The entrance led to a white-covered aisle, ready for the bride-to-be. The setting and her mommy were both absolutely beautiful. Tina was a cute little flower girl that day. She walked proudly in front of the bride, carefully selecting each rose petal, gingerly plucking one at a time out of the specially decorated basket, and tossing it to the aisle floor in front of the beautiful bride—her mommy. Tina felt very special.

Tina had known Larry all her life and even though she didn't have anything against him, she didn't initially accept him as her father. No one could take the place of Bill, the daddy Tina so desperately wanted to love her. Larry and his two children moved into the Miller's small, three-bedroom house. They put three boys in one bedroom, three girls in one bedroom, and their parents stayed in the master bedroom. All eight of them had one very small bathroom to share.

Tina's biological father, Bill, died when she was eleven. Martha and Larry gathered all six of the kids into the den, and explained Bill had died after falling asleep in his garage with the car running. Tina could feel laughter welling up inside, and ran up to the kitchen to hide the fact she felt like laughing instead of crying. Tina really couldn't remember much about Bill, so what did it matter if he had died? She felt ashamed of her reaction. "Shouldn't I feel like crying? He was my father," Tina thought. Perhaps she didn't cry because she hadn't seen or heard from him since she was six, or maybe it was the simple shock of it all.

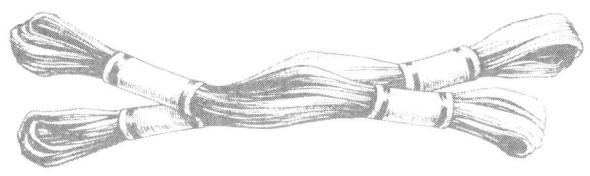

No matter how invisible we may feel or think we are to those around us, God truly sees.

Then she called the name of the LORD
who spoke to her, You-Are-the-God-Who-Sees;
for she said, "Have I also here seen
Him who sees me?"
(Genesis 16:13)

The LORD looks from heaven;
He sees all the sons of men.
From the place of His dwelling He looks
On all the inhabitants of the earth;
He fashions their hearts individually;
He considers all their works.
(Psalm 33:13-15)

What shades of PINK is God revealing about you that will be part of your life tapestry? [156]

_____
_____
_____
_____
_____
_____
_____
_____
_____
_____
_____
_____
_____
_____
_____
_____
_____
_____
_____

God can open your eyes to see through the lies you hear within; lies that you're insignificant, ugly or "stupid." You can stand upon the truth that, if you are a child of God, you are precious in His sight.

*But you **are** a chosen generation, a royal priesthood, a holy nation, His own special people, that you may proclaim the praises of Him who called you out of darkness into His marvelous light; who once **were** not a people but **are** now the people of God, who had not obtained mercy but now have obtained mercy.*
(1 Peter 2:9-10)

Behold what manner of love the Father has bestowed on us, that we should be called children of God! Therefore the world does not know us, because it did not know Him. Beloved, now we are children of God; and it has not yet been revealed what we shall be, but we know that when He is revealed, we shall be like Him, for we shall see Him as He is. And everyone who has this hope in Him purifies himself, just as He is pure.
(1 John 3:1-3)

What PINK threads of truth is God weaving for you right now? [157]

_____
_____
_____
_____
_____
_____
_____
_____
_____
_____
_____
_____
_____

Tina's biological father may have abandoned her—your own father may have abandoned you—but God will never leave you, nor forsake you.

*No man **shall be** able to stand before you all the days of your life; as I was with Moses, **so** I will be with you. I will not leave you nor forsake you. (Joshua 1:5)*

*Sing to God, sing praises to His name; Extol Him who rides on the clouds, By His name YAH, And rejoice before Him. A father of the fatherless, a defender of widows, **Is** God in His holy habitation. (Psalm 68:4-5)*

*Let **your** conduct **be** without covetousness; **be** content with such things as you have. For He Himself has said, "I will never leave you nor forsake you." So we may boldly say: "The Lord **is** my helper; I will not fear. What can man do to me?" (Hebrews 13:5-6)*

What PINK promises of God are being woven into your life tapestry? *158/159*

_____
_____
_____
_____
_____
_____
_____
_____
_____
_____
_____
_____
_____
_____
_____
_____
_____
_____

BLUE
Blurring the Lines

Tina grew up knowing Larry, who would later become her stepdad, since the day she was born. Bill lived with Larry and his family after Bill's mother passed away. As a matter of fact, Martha, Bill, and Larry all attended the same high school together. Bill's father was working as a prop master for Paramount Pictures at the time his mother passed away and was rarely home, so Bill moved in with Larry. Larry was an only child and lived in a huge house in Palos Verdes with his parents. The stories about the teenage antics of these boys are quite entertaining: riding horses (more like horsing around), cruising in their souped-up hot rods, climbing trees, cutting school, and simply being adventurous, mischievous boys.

Larry married his first wife, Mary, after knowing her for only a few months. Larry played the saxophone and, more often than not, was out nights playing gigs. He even went on tour to Australia with Chubby Checker and the Peppermints; he was that good! One night, while Larry was out on a gig, his wife Mary was violently murdered, in front of their two children. Tina's stepbrother, Rick, was only three, and Maggie, her stepsister, was six when they witnessed their mother brutally beaten to death with a croquet mallet. Rick blames himself to this day, holding onto feelings of guilt because he didn't do anything to stop the man who killed her; but he was only three!

Maggie and Rick told Tina the horrifying story of what they remember about how their mom was murdered and all the blood they saw—a very scary story for little Tina to hear. They told her a strange man had knocked on Mary's bedroom window. Rick was asleep next to her in bed. Mary opened the window to let the man in. She must have recognized him to have done so. He then proceeded to beat Mary to death, hitting her over the head multiple times with a croquet mallet. Maggie and Rick, awakened by the screaming, both witnessed the horrific murder of their mother.

One night, not long after Maggie had told little Tina about what happened to Mary, Tina was alone in her bedroom when someone knocked on the bedroom window. Tina was absolutely terrified! She jumped out of bed, ran down the hall, through the kitchen, and down the two small stairs leading to the den where her mom and Larry were watching television. Try as she might to tell them someone was at her window, she was so terribly frightened, not a sound would come out of her mouth. Just then, Maggie came in from the backyard, laughing hysterically. Tina didnt find it funny, for sure, and she grew up afraid to go to sleep at night fearing someone was going to come through the window and kill her.

Mary had been rather promiscuous, and didn't set any boundaries with her children, or men, for that matter. Her promiscuity is probably what led to her murder. Her daughter, Maggie, spoke to Tina a lot about sex and boys' bodies when Tina was still too young to really understand. Maggie followed in her mother's footsteps, and would often sneak out her bedroom window at night, not coming home until the following morning. Maggie was also hard of hearing, and had a learning disability, so boys took advantage her. Tina's household had no sexual boundaries. As a matter of fact, from the time Tina was in junior high, sex was a frequent topic of conversation.

Rick and Tina had a childhood crush on one another. Tina had no idea the ramifications their innocent little crush would have later in life. In the beginning, after her mom and Larry married, Tina still didn't really consider Rick as a brother. One Father's Day, a few years into their marriage, Tina decided to finally accept Larry as her "father." She couldn't wait to see the look on her "dad's" face when he opened the Father's Day card she got him, and read the words she had written, "I love you, dad." Calling Larry dad was a big step for Tina; one she remembers quite vividly. At the same time, Tina also began to see Rick as her brother, rather than a boyfriend, and her childhood crush subsided. So, not surprisingly, when Rick attempted to have sex with her, it brought confusion and uncertainty. She had no idea what he was doing. They were both young and Tina was at a complete loss. She knew her brother wouldn't intentionally try to hurt her. This incident began to blur the lines between love and sex for Tina.

Tina had no foundation to learn how to separate sex from love. I'm sure there are women reading this who can relate. How often do we base our value on how we look, how skinny or fit we are (or aren't), how sexually appealing we are (or aren't). Thankfully, God doesn't base our value on such things. He created us, each one, unique and special. Think of how wonderful it would be to look into a mirror without picking yourself apart!

Ask God to show you what you look like through His eyes; to give you the ability to see yourself, not as the world views you, but as He actually sees you. He will answer your prayer so when you look in the mirror you may actually see someone that beautiful; someone fearfully and wonderfully made by almighty God Himself! (*Psalm 139:14*). Tina learned the lesson and, although she may not always see beauty, she knows without a shadow of a doubt God is changing her from the inside out, giving her new eyes, and freeing her from the lies she listened to for so many years.

I will praise You, for I am fearfully
and *wonderfully made;*
Marvelous are Your works,
And ***that*** *my soul knows very well.*
(Psalm 139:14)

Sex does not equate to love; let no one convince you it does. Having sex outside of marriage affects your innermost being—your soul.

*Do you not know that your bodies are members of Christ? Shall I then take the members of Christ and make **them** members of a harlot? Certainly not! Or do you not know that he who is joined to a harlot is one body **with** her? For "the two," He says, "shall become one flesh." But he who is joined to the Lord is one spirit **with Him.***
(1 Corinthians 6:15-17)

What hues of BLUE is God revealing you need to turn away from? [160]

_____
_____
_____
_____
_____
_____
_____
_____
_____
_____
_____
_____
_____
_____
_____
_____
_____
_____
_____
_____
_____
_____

For this is the will of God, your sanctification:
that you should abstain from sexual immorality;
that each of you should know how to possess his own
vessel in sanctification and honor (1 Thessalonians 4:3-4)

Are there more hues of BLUE that God wants to add to your tapestry? [160]

Our value is not based upon our looks. God created each one of us to be special. We are of great value to God, our Creator.

> *For You formed my inward parts;*
> *You covered me in my mother's womb.*
> *I will praise You, for I am fearfully*
> ***and*** *wonderfully made;*
> *Marvelous are Your works,*
> *And **that** my soul knows very well.*
> *My frame was not hidden from You,*
> *When I was made in secret,*
> ***And*** *skillfully wrought*
> *in the lowest parts of the earth.*
> *(Psalm 139:13-15)*

What beautiful shades of BLUE is your Creator adding to the tapestry of you? [161]

GREY
Choking from the Smoke

Rick loved playing with his chemistry set when he was a kid. Science, especially anything concerning the ocean, greatly intrigued him. One Saturday, eleven-year-old Tina was playing in her room when she heard horrifying screams coming from down the hall. She ran out of her bedroom to see what the all commotion was about. No one would let Tina near her brother's bedroom. Rick had accidentally set the room on fire.! He was playing with his chemistry set and, while lighting the Bunsen burner, knocked it over and unintentionally set the bedroom floor ablaze. The older kids, a few neighbors, and Larry frantically pulled a garden hose through the bedroom window to put the fire out. They successfully extinguished the fire, but Rick was still screaming; something about his leg. Rick's leg was on fire. Martha and Larry rushed Rick to the hospital, where doctors informed them that their son had sustained extensive third degree burns down the entire length of his right shin.

Unfortunately, the couple couldn't afford the skin grafts doctors recommended at the time. Rick suffered for years with his burn constantly becoming an open sore at the slightest bump. Although Tina didn't see Rick's leg actually on fire, she did see the wound when the bandage was changed. The ghastly sight of his burn is something she hasn't forgotten. Years later, as an adult, Rick's wound had become so dire, the doctors told him that without the skin grafts they would have to amputate his leg. So Rick finally broke down and had the skin graft done.

Fire is a dangerous thing in the hands of a child.

Now in junior high, Tina was home after school one Friday, looking forward to a weekend of fun at the beach, when her optimism was stripped away by the news brought by a knock on the door. Her sister Shawn's best friend, Emily, had committed suicide. Sitting with the family in shock and grief, Shawn recalled Emily being so happy, so at peace that day at school. "Why did she do such a thing?" Shawn asked. The loss was devastating for everyone who knew Emily. Emily's was the first funeral Tina remembers attending. Tina walked into the church filled with family and friends and, as soon as she saw all the beautiful flowers, broke down sobbing. Emily was a beautiful girl, and kindhearted to all. What had made Emily so sad, so lost, so broken?

Tina's older brother, Todd, had a friend who lived down the street whom she considered cute. His name was Kevin, and Tina had a huge crush on him. One summer, Kevin and his family planned to spend a few weeks in Mexico, and set off in their camper-trailer. Mexico wasn't as dangerous then as it is today. As a matter of fact, Tina's entire family used to drive down to Tijuana in their Volkswagen van just to go shopping, since you could find some great deals down there. On their family's trip, Kevin had a bad asthma attack during their drive down. Kevin's inhaler was back in the trailer they were pulling. He didn't want them to pull over and stop, because it would slow down the trip. Being a stubborn, adventurous teen, Kevin decided he could get to the trailer by traversing over the trailer hitch from the camper to the trailer while they were driving. Kevin and his family never made it to Mexico. Kevin fell, and was accidentally run over and killed by his own family. His parents must have been devastated. Tina had another funeral to attend, still only in junior high.

Tina's stepgrandpa, Barry, was quite a character. He was the strong, silent type. Rarely would you see him without a cigarette in his mouth. Barry tried to quit smoking after his first heart attack, but couldn't. He cut down quite a bit, and even stopped eating salt, but still couldn't go an entire day without smoking. Tina's family visited him and her stepgrandma, Ruth, down at the boat nearly every weekend. Ruth cooked great dinners but, for someone who enjoys salt as much as Tina, the meals tasted bland.

Barry died of congestive heart failure when Tina was still in junior high. His body was cremated. The boat ride wasn't such a happy time when they took Barry's ashes to be spread in the sea. Tina's family had not attended any sort of church service, nor did they pray, or even discuss God or spirituality and religion, at this point in their lives.

Tina experienced a lot of death and sadness at an early age, but would learn later in life that even those heartbreaking experiences can be used by the Lord to help others in their time of loss and grief.

*And we know that all things work together for good to those who love God, to those who are the called according to **His** purpose.   (Romans 8:28)*

Are there GREY threads in your current life tapestry? [162]

_____

_____

_____

_____

_____

_____

_____

_____

No matter how sad we may become during the dark times in our lives, nothing should ever cause you to consider taking your own life. It's a selfish act which leaves our loved ones empty and, without God, in despair. In Christ, there is always hope.

*For I consider that the sufferings of this present time are not worthy **to be compared** with the glory which shall be revealed in us.   (Romans 8:18)*

"And I say to you, My friends, do not be afraid of those who kill the body, and after that have no more that they can do. But I will show you whom you should fear: Fear Him who, after He has killed, has power to cast into hell; yes, I say to you, fear Him!
Are not five sparrows sold for two copper coins? And not one of them is forgotten before God. But the very hairs of your head are all numbered. Do not fear therefore; you are of more value than many sparrows."   (Luke 12:4-7)

What does God promise in the midst the GREY threads? [163]

_____

_____

_____

_____

_____

_____

_____

_____

_____

_____

_____

_____

_____

GREEN
Entertaining Deception

In high school, Tina took up skateboarding, which was quite rare for girls back then. Tina's friend Laura was the only other girl in the area who skateboarded. Laura was one of a handful of female pro skateboarders in the 1970s. She skated on the Logan[6] Skateboard Team, and continues the legend today. As a matter of fact, Laura was inducted into the Skateboarding Hall of Fame in 2013. Tina and Laura used to go skateboarding in La Costa with Bruce Logan, of Logan Earth Ski, Tony Alva and others.

Tina's first time skateboarding in an empty pool was quite memorable for her. Because skate parks had yet to be created, Tina and her skater friends would often go hunting for empty pools. Most of the time Tina sat on the sidelines and watched the boys pool skate, but as she became a better, bolder skateboarder, Tina wanted to experience skating a pool herself.

Looking for new homes under construction was one way to find an empty pool, and was how they found one on this particular day. Todd, Tina, and one of Todd's friends, Randy, climbed the fence, and off they went. Todd skated first—down, up, hit the coping, and back down again. Next was Randy; he didn't quite hit the coping, but he still enjoyed his ride. Then Tina went—down, up, around, and down again.

"What a rush!" she said, with a huge smile on her face as she climbed the stairs out of the shallow end of the pool to let Todd have his turn. Tina couldn't wait for her next run, and the next, and next, each a little higher than the previous ride.

Sadly for them, it began to drizzle—you just don't skateboard in a pool in the rain. So, to keep from slipping and being injured, Todd told them they needed to head home. Tina just had to get one more run in so, when Todd turned around, off she went—and down she came, hard.

Tina slipped and fell right on her bottom, using her hand to break the fall. Ouch! Her wrist immediately began to swell and was throbbing in pain. Tina didn't make a fuss though. She had a crush on Randy and didn't want him to see her as wimpy. They climbed back over the fence and skated home. Tina's wrist was hurting pretty bad when Randy exclaimed, "Your wrist can't be broken or you would be crying by now." That made Tina feel strong and neither Todd nor she said anything about the injury to their parents. They had been trespassing and didn't want to get in trouble.

The following day, Tina's wrist was much more swollen and bruised, and she couldn't move it. She showed it to Todd and they decided they had to tell their parents. Her parents took Tina to the doctor, where she had her first x-ray. Sure enough, her wrist was broken. It was her first "war" wound! They gave her one of the first waterproof casts (plastic with holes), and she wore it proudly, knowing she could brag about how she broke her wrist when classmates asked at school the next day.

One night after school, Tina got a call from a friend of Laura's brother who was looking for girl skaters to work on a television show called *Family*. Tina's parents let her take a couple of days off school to work on the show. Martha drove Tina to the set and stayed with her there while they were shooting. Tina wasn't quite eighteen yet, so a parent had to be present for her to work.

Tina had been cast as a skateboarding stunt double for Genie Francis in her first television role. Genie is most famous for her role as Laura on the popular soap opera *General Hospital*. Although Tina and her family had been to Universal Studios, this was her first experience actually working on a film or television set, and she enjoyed it. They used her a lot, since Genie didn't know how to ride a skateboard. Tina befriended many of the cast members who were all very nice to her.

Famous pro-skateboarder, Laura, wasn't too happy about the whole thing. She was a much better skateboarder than Tina, but was stuck in a trailer with the school tutor doing schoolwork, because Kristy McNichol, whom she was doubling for, knew how to ride a skateboard and wanted to do her own skating. They took quite a few takes for the big skateboard race scene between Kristy and Genie. Tina's right knee totally locked up during one of the takes (television lingo for shots, as in photography) and she couldn't straighten or bend it.

The medic on location wanted Tina to stop skating. But just as he was looking it over, her knee freed up. Because it didn't really hurt, Tina kept on skating. Her knee didn't lock up again for the remainder of the shoot, but it did periodically in the weeks following the shoot, so to the doctor she went for her second x-ray. Part of the leg bone connecting the knee had chipped off, and was getting stuck behind the kneecap, preventing her knee from bending. This condition is called osteochondritis dissecans. Initially, they expected the piece of bone to disintegrate since it wasn't getting any nutrients, but that never happened. So, the following year, when Tina was eighteen, she had her first surgery. The surgeon removed the piece of bone and drilled holes in the leg bone it had broken off from so it would get more circulation and not reoccur.

Tina didn't know then, but film production was in her blood. As an adult, she absolutely loves being on set. To most people, sitting around for hours and hours doing nothing while the crew relights, repositions cameras, and other various work required before starting on the next scene, is more boring than it is fun. The passion Tina has for it probably came from Bill's side of the family. Her great uncle, Ray, was a set director who won three Academy Awards for Best Art Direction for his work on *Samson and Delilah*, *Sunset Boulevard*, and *Cleopatra*. He was nominated for nine more Oscars, including ones for *The Ten Commandments*, *Breakfast at Tiffany's*, and *The Greatest Story Ever Told*. He also worked on the majority of John Wayne's films, becoming good friends with him, an even had cameos in a few movies. He was quite a character and, although Tina only met him a few times, she will never forget him.

One of the stories he told her was about how he had gone to Egypt to get ideas for the set of *The Ten Commandments*. He had a vial of Egyptian sand and some water from the Nile River to bring back to the United States so he could match colors and design the set just right. But he was stopped at the airport, and nearly arrested and thrown in prison, simply for attempting to bring sand and water out of the country.

Additionally, Tina's grandfather on her biological father's side worked in the film industry, as a prop master for Paramount Pictures. If you ask Tina what it is that interests her about film and television, she'll tell you "Working on a movie or television show is like putting a huge puzzle together. It takes thousands of little pieces that, once fully assembled, can make a wonderfully entertaining, moving picture that tells an interesting story."

Tina worked at Mattel Toys in her early twenties, and ended up being the token hand model in nearly all the commercials shot during her four years working in the promotional services department. She was sent by Mattel to numerous locations to take care of the prototype toys being used during a commercial shoot—she was the "toy wrangler."

By happenstance, on the very first commercial Tina ever worked on, the producers were concerned about the possibility of incurring the additional expense of carrying the shoot into another day. They had to send the child actors home because child labor laws restricted the number of hours they were allowed to work. All the scenes that didn't feature a child's face were shot with a hand model but they didn't have enough hand models for all the shots they still needed. That's when someone noticed how small Tina's hands were, and the rest is history. Mattel added Tina's name to most of the call sheets for their commercials. She even had the privilege of working with the director of photography for *Close Encounters of the Third Kind*, Vilmosh Zigmond. Tina had numerous opportunities to work in the film industry, but simply couldn't bear the thought of not having a steady paycheck, or knowing when or where the next job would come.

As mentioned in the PINK chapter, Tina's biological father remarried and had a son named William, after his dad. After his mother passed away, William made a point to find his family. He called Tina's mom and, not long after their first conversation, he flew to California to meet them. He shared a lot about Bill, his line of work and how he didn't die the way they were told. William insinuated that Bill might not be dead at all—what a shock for Tina! The thought her biological father might actually still be alive devastated her. Especially considering she grew up without him, and he never reached out to his children as they were growing up. The stories William told became rather bizarre. Stories about Bill being in the CIA, warning them they all needed to be careful, people were watching them, etc. Quite frankly, everyone thought William was off his rocker.

Fast forward six years and, with some encouragement, Tina decided to dig a little deeper into the tales told by her half-brother suggesting her father might still be alive. The more research she did into Bill's work, his death, his life, the more questions arose. William had given Todd copies of documents which actually validated some of the stories. Tina decided, in order to keep some emotional distance from the whole thing, to treat it as a story, and, at the prompting of a friend who worked in the film industry, began writing all the information down in the form of a screenplay.

One Thanksgiving, Tina was at her parents' house when she used the after-dinner conversation as an opportunity to ask Larry and Martha questions about Bill. Tina was sharing with them some of her ideas for the screenplay, prefacing the stories were fictional, "Hollywood hype," and not to be taken seriously or personally. In the story, Tina wanted to make her dad out to be the good guy, so her idea was for him to be with the Japanese woman he committed adultery with while married to her mom only to extrapolate information for the U.S. government, by order of the CIA.

After Tina shared her story idea, Larry proceeded to tell her Bill actually did work for the CIA. Years before, Bill told Larry he had joined a religious organization with the Japanese woman while he was on a specific CIA assignment. After that Thanksgiving, Todd sent Tina copies of some of the documents William gave him and right there, in black and white, it clearly stated, "Membership in this organization was maintained in cooperation with the Office of Special Investigation, Hq. 5th Air Force, Fuchu Air Station, Japan."

Tina couldn't believe it, exclaiming, "WOW! Are you kidding me?" Her story ideas were turning out to be more fact than fiction. Tina posted a few story lines on Facebook and was contacted by William's half-brother, Don. He wanted to share some information with Tina. As an older adult, Don's curiosity about his stepfather (Tina's dad) had been piqued by memories of his past. Don is a retired sheriff, so Tina felt the information he shared was credible.

Because of Bill's job, the family had to move around a lot. They lived in the Bahamas, San Salvador, and other countries, but their main residence was Florida, since Bill worked at Kennedy Space Center for NASA. Bill told his second wife, Bertha, he worked for the CIA. Don told Tina about times when he and his siblings would have to leave the property when Bill's friends, dressed in suits, cleanly pressed white shirts, and black ties, would visit. Don also recounted a memory of Bill showing him pictures of a Russian and a Chinese agent. When Bill supposedly died, they didn't even have a funeral. Don was not convinced of Bill's death.

So, what was Tina supposed to do with such information? She lived her entire life never knowing her father, and now she learned he might not even be dead? If he was alive, why didn't he ever try to contact his daughter; especially now that she was an adult? Regardless, it made for a very compelling story.

Tina need not concern herself with trying to find out whether her dad is alive or dead. It really doesn't matter either way. She knows God, not her father, is in control of her life. As we make the Lord the center of our lives, our peace and joy is no longer dependent upon our dad's involvement (or lack thereof) in our lives. In Christ we find our peace. In Christ we find love complete. In and through Jesus comes absolute acceptance and unconditional love.

*Come now, you who say, "Today or tomorrow we will go to such and such a city, spend a year there, buy and sell, and make a profit"; whereas you do not know what **will happen** tomorrow."*
(James 4:13-14)

What GREEN threads are being woven into your tapestry you right now? [164]

_____
_____
_____
_____
_____
_____
_____
_____
_____
_____
_____

But indeed, O man, who are you to reply against God? Will the thing formed say to him who formed it, "Why have you made me like this?" Does not the potter have power over the clay, from the same lump to make one vessel for honor and another for dishonor?
(Romans 9:20-21)

'Ah, Lord GOD! Behold, You have made the heavens and the earth by Your great power and outstretched arm. There is nothing too hard for You.
(Jeremiah 32:17)

Are there additional shades of GREEN being woven into your tapestry right now? [164]

_____
_____
_____
_____
_____
_____
_____
_____
_____
_____
_____
_____
_____
_____
_____
_____
_____
_____
_____
_____
_____

TURQUOISE
Drowning in a Sea of Lies

Growing up, Tina was shy and insecure, so she immersed herself in a world of art and creativity. As a young girl, she was always drawing. Her artwork consisted mostly of flowers with faces, evolving to sunsets, surfers, and waves in high school, then to portraits and abstract design in college and into her adult years. She took any and all art classes she could. Her siblings were also artistic. Her sister, Shawn, was an amazing artist. Shawn's use of primary colors and black in paintings of seemingly normal subject matter evoked unexpected emotion in nearly all who viewed her paintings. Shawn was such a fine artist, she was offered a full scholarship at the California Institute of the Arts, one of the top ranking art schools. But Shawn opted to get married instead. Tina won her share of awards for her artwork, but she didn't consider herself to be the same caliber artist as her sister.

Tina was rather awkward, tomboyish and shy in high school. Influenced by her older brother, Todd, and his cute surfer friends, she loved going body surfing, snow skiing, water-skiing, skateboarding, and, in her adult years, added dirt bike (motorcycle) riding and surfing to her list of outdoor activities.

Tina's senior year of high school marked the beginning of her history of bad relationships. To start with, she fell in love with a boy named Jay, who secretly had a girlfriend. Tina was at a high school dance, standing among the many girls eagerly waiting to be asked to dance, when a tough girl approached her and asked, "Hey, do you know Jay?" Tina responded in the affirmative and the tough girl threatened to beat Tina up. Tina was scared and didn't know what to do. Right in the nick of time, Todd walked up, told the toughy to leave Tina alone, and they left the dance hall.

The tough girl was Jay's girlfriend. Tina had no idea he had a girlfriend and was absolutely devastated, especially considering the fact that Jay was her first real boyfriend and she thought she was really in love.

Tina equated sex with love. She had no boundaries, and thought sex was an OK, and even necessary, part of any relationship with a man. Because of these erroneous beliefs of hers, Tina thought she was truly in love with Jay and, wanting him to love her back, she allowed him to have sex with her. She was eighteen at the time. So the first boy Tina fell in love with had lied to her, having another girlfriend all along. This was the first in a long line of relationships Tina had with men for whom Tina was not their only love.

After Jay was Travis. Travis was as good a dancer as Tina and they made a great couple on the dance floor. In the days of *Saturday Night Fever*, Tina and Travis were the ones to watch. Although Travis claimed to love Tina, he treated her more like a commodity, someone to help make him look good. It seemed to Tina as though she could never do anything right for him. She never wore the right thing or looked the right way but, since she had little self-worth to begin with, the relationship fit her just fine, fitting right in with her thought patterns of "I'm ugly and can't do anything right." Travis left Tina for another girl, reinforcing Tina's thoughts of worthlessness.

Throughout her relationship with Travis, a boy named Dean had been pushing her to go out with him every time he saw her. After Travis left Tina, it was Dean who was there to pick up the pieces. He was her shoulder to cry on, and she ended up dating him for over two years. This time, Tina thought, Dean was "the one" she would marry. He treated her so much better than the others. He bought her gifts and flowers, and would write her nice cards and put notes on her car. Tina took notice when the relationship began to change. Dean wasn't calling her as much, and they weren't spending as much time together as they had been. She immediately thought he must be cheating on her, but had no real proof—until the day she was skating with her best friend, Mindy, down on the strand in Hermosa Beach. There was Dean kissing a girl, right there in front of her own two eyes! Tina was hurt and angry but just kept skating. She was talking to Mindy about it when a guy skated up next to them and started talking to them. His name was Mark, and he was visiting for the summer from Canada. Tina explained to this complete stranger what had just happened, and asked if he'd mind skating with them to pass by where Dean was with the other girl. Mark happily agreed, and put his arm around Tina as they skated by in plain sight of Dean and his new love interest. This incident started the end of Tina's relationship with Dean and the beginning of her relationship with Mark.

Dean called Tina multiple times every day crying, telling her how Mark didn't love her, and how Dean and Tina were meant to be together. He apologized for cheating on her, which confused her and made it more difficult for her to leave him. One day when Tina got home from the beach, she found out her pet rabbit, Benjamin, had died. Benjamin was a huge, lop-eared rabbit who was actually more like a dog than a rabbit. He would come when called, and never tried to escape from the backyard. In order to try to persuade her to get back together with him, after Benjamin died, Dean bought Tina a Chow Chow, her favorite breed of dog at the time; but that didn't change Tina's mind.

Mark's time in California was coming to an end so, not wanting to leave the relationship, he invited Tina to go back to Canada with him. Considering the circumstances and the fact it was summer break, Tina's parents thought it was a good idea. Tina spent two months that summer in beautiful British Columbia. They camped on Vancouver Island where they fed deer by hand. Tina even witnessed a mother bear and her two cubs run across the freeway on one of their drives. Now there's something you'd never see in LA! They also went to the Calgary Stampede, Alberta, Canada's roughest rodeo festival, which was absolutely crazy! After two months in Canada it was time for Tina to go home. Mark had treated her with great kindness and seemed to really care about her, but she had to get back to school if she was ever going to graduate from El Camino College, so she ended their relationship.

Not having the sort of love and acceptance she so craved from her biological father caused Tina to seek love and acceptance elsewhere, and she went from one boyfriend to the next. But, there is one relationship she opened the door to which was good—her relationship with Christ.

Tina's relationship with Christ began during the Jesus movement in the 1970s. Her brother, Todd, was dating a girl who was a born-again Christian. She invited Tina to join them one night for a Christian outreach concert at Calvary Chapel of Costa Mesa. The Maranatha concert moved Tina very much. Toward the end, there was an invitation to accept Jesus Christ as your Lord and Savior. Tina joined many others in walking to the front of the stage and, in tears, prayed the "sinner's prayer," asking Jesus into her heart.

Though Tina had made this emotional decision, she was still self-centered, and continued seeking love and acceptance elsewhere. She had yet to fully understand how much God Himself loves her. Furthermore, no one had ever taken her through the Bible or told her the significance of Jesus in her life, so she never fully realized the importance of what she had done, or what the sinner's prayer really meant. The Christian outreach concert was the beginning of Jesus pulling her toward Him. She went to church a few times, but certainly wasn't living a life of obedience. She hadn't fully repented of her sin.

Many people have a false sense of having a free ticket to heaven because they say a prayer. Tina was one of them. She thought she was assured of heaven because she prayed and asked Jesus into her heart. But she continued living a life controlled by sin and selfishness, thinking all the while God would forgive her sin. It's not that God won't forgive the sin of a repentant heart, but praying to ask Jesus into our heart does not give us license to sin. No magical prayer immediately gives us the right to heaven. If we truly realize all Jesus did for us, our desires change, and we want to live a life pleasing to Him who suffered a horrific death for us.

Jesus reveals the depths of our sin, and the fact that living a life of sin is evidence we have not fully submitted to Him. Instead, it's evidence we have not truly been born-again—we're really not a Christian, a follower of Christ. When we realize the full gravity of our sin, we realize we need to fully submit and put our trust and faith in Jesus. Turning away from our old sinful ways is evidence we have been born-again as followers of Christ. Only Jesus can save us from the sin we are so easily ensnared[7] by. Only in Him, and through the indwelling of the Holy Spirit, do we have the strength to live a life of obedience.

What if Tina had known then what she knows now? She trusts God has a plan for her life, and has permitted what she's gone through for a reason. May the Lord use her story to prompt you, His beloved, to turn away from sin, and toward the Savior.

Tina began seeking love and acceptance through relationships, when pure love and acceptance can only be found in Christ.

*The Lord is not slack concerning **His** promise, as some count slackness, but is longsuffering toward us, not willing that any should perish but that all should come to repentance.* (2 Peter 3:9)

What is your TURQUOISE shade of love right now? [165]

_____
_____
_____
_____
_____
_____

*And you **He made alive**, who were dead in trespasses and sins, in which you once walked according to the course of this world, according to the prince of the power of the air, the spirit who now works in the sons of disobedience, among whom also we all once conducted ourselves in the lusts of our flesh, fulfilling the desires of the flesh and of the mind, and were by nature children of wrath, just as the others. But God, who is rich in mercy, because of His great love with which He loved us, even when we were dead in trespasses, made us alive together with Christ (by grace you have been saved), and raised **us** up together, and made us sit together in the heavenly **places** in Christ Jesus, that in the ages to come He might show the exceeding riches of His grace in His kindness toward us in Christ Jesus. (Ephesians 2:1-7)*

What TURQUOISE threads are God weaving into your tapestry to reveal how much He loves you? [165]

_____

_____

_____

_____

_____

_____

_____

_____

_____

_____

_____

_____

_____

_____

_____

_____

_____

Tina thought she was a Christian, but continued living in sin. A true believer no longer desires a life of sin; rather he seeks repentance and change.

"He who has My commandments and keeps them,
it is he who loves Me. And he who loves Me
will be loved by My Father, and I will love him
and manifest Myself to him."   *(John 14:21)*

"As the Father loved Me, I also have loved you;
abide in My love. If you keep My commandments,
you will abide in My love, just as I have kept
My Father's commandments and abide in His love."
(John 15:9-10)

Is there anything you need to do so God can weave more TURQUOISE of His abiding love into the tapestry of your life? [166]

_____
_____
_____
_____
_____
_____
_____
_____
_____
_____
_____
_____
_____
_____
_____
_____
_____
_____

*Therefore we make it our aim, whether present or absent, to be well pleasing to Him. For we must all appear before the judgment seat of Christ, that each one may receive the things **done** in the body, according to what he has done, whether good or bad. Knowing, therefore, the terror of the Lord, we persuade men; but we are well known to God, and I also trust are well known in your consciences.*
(2 Corinthians 5:9-11)

What compels you in the TURQUOISE threads to live as the Lord calls you to live? [167]

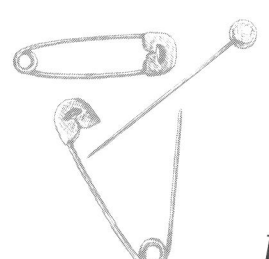

SCARLET
Burning Misery

Tina graduated high school in 1978, with a 3.8 GPA. She had the privilege of taking nothing but art classes the majority of her senior year, since she had completed all her general education classes. Because she won numerous awards for her artwork throughout Jr. high and high school, Tina continued studying art at El Camino College. She was the first in her family to earn any level of college degree. She started working at Mattel Toys while she was still in school, but managed to finish by attending classes at night.

Tina's interest in photography came after her boyfriend, Dean, loaned her a camera. One of her photography teachers recognized Tina's creative eye. He and his wife treated her with great kindness inviting her to their home after school for dinner. Her teacher took Tina under his wing and taught her how to use his equipment. He even allowed her use of his photography studio. He also surreptitiously submitted Tina for Robert D. Keitel Memorial Scholarship for excellence in photography. Tina was awarded the small scholarship but had yet to fully believe that God created her with an excellent eye for photography.

In Tina's second year of college she landed in the hospital after an extended period of continual bleeding (female issues) resulted in major blood loss. Only when she fainted during a phone call to her doctor, did he finally decide perhaps the bleeding should be taken seriously enough to send her to the hospital. Tina was so weak she couldn't even sit upright during the short car ride to the hospital. Tina had lost nearly half of her blood, and was given four blood transfusions, but the bleeding didn't stop. The hospital called in a specialist to examine Tina and he recommended a minor surgical procedure to stop the bleeding. As they wheeled her into the operating room, Tina noticed a cross above the door which inspired her to pray. Tina prayed the Lord's Prayer, and promised God she would stop the sexual sin with her boyfriend if she got better. Tina thought God was punishing her for her sin. Though she didn't realize just how serious her condition was at the time—Tina was near death—she was fearful nonetheless.

Following the procedure, the bleeding stopped and, after four days in the hospital, she was released. Although she attributed the fact she was still alive to God, she didn't follow through on her promise to Him. Tina didn't change her lifestyle, and continued living in sin. She loved God (or so she thought), but she had not yet fully repented of her sin. Tina should have never made a promise she couldn't keep. Deep down inside, she had yet to accept the truth that God loved her. Tina continued to seek love and acceptance elsewhere, even after the Lord saved her life—literally. The illness set Tina back a bit, but she managed to graduate from El Camino and achieve her associate's degree.

In high school, Tina had a good friend named Candy with whom she used to go skateboarding. Tina hadn't spoken to or seen Candy much after they graduated from high school. Home one night after work, Tina's mom called and told her she had heard Candy's name mentioned on the news. Concerned, Martha told Tina how she had been watching television when an urgent news story broke about an explosion at the Torrance oil refinery. The explosion caused a horrendous fire that killed three people, seriously injuring others. As soon as she hung up with her mom, Tina called Candy but got no answer. Tina called Candy's parents. Her voice filled with emotion, Candy's mother told Tina that her one and only child, Candy, was in the hospital. Tina's friend was, in fact, the same Candy mentioned on the news. Candy was driving past the refinery when fumes from her car mixed with fumes caused by an unexplained fuel leak from the refinery. The deadly mixture caused a huge fireball to explode Candy's car, and trigger a massive fire. Candy was hospitalized, with over 80 percent of her body burned. Tina didn't visit Candy in the hospital. Tina simply couldn't bear to see Candy burned so badly, suffering such excruciating pain. Candy died four days after the accident. Tina didn't attend Candy's funeral.

From an early age, Tina experienced a great deal of death and loss, so she feared getting close to anyone lest they either leave her or die. Candy's death was the first in a series of deaths which Tina didn't attend memorials for. Perhaps she was tired of all the loss and, in an attempt to avoid it, simply didn't say good-bye.

Now in her early twenties, Tina had yet another boyfriend, Bobby. He was an authentic rodeo rider, competing in bronco riding. In the days of *Urban Cowboy*, who could resist? Seeing Bobby ride was really something, but Tina feared for his life every time she watched him. Bobby lived on beautiful Balboa Island with his brother and sister-in-law, and worked as a deck hand on one of the boats his brother tended. Tina spent most of her weekends with Bobby in Balboa, to get away from the volatile relationship she had with her mom.

Tina was out buying some artistic window decals to put on her little blue VW bug one day and when she got home her mom ran out yelling and asking where Tina had been. Martha had obviously been waiting for her daughter. Tina thought her mom would start the same screaming she knew so well—profanities and expletives about what she had done wrong, and how she wanted Tina out of the house.

Instead, Martha told her Bobby had been in an accident. Bobby, his brother, and some friends had been out on their boat drinking. Someone threw a beer to Bobby and when he reached out to catch the beer can, he missed and it fell into the water. Bobby dove in after the can of beer and came up face first into the boat's propeller. His face was torn up by the prop. It also broke his jaw and knocked out some of his teeth. Although Tina and Bobby hadn't been getting along very well, Tina still cared enough about him to spend the majority of her time that summer nursing him back to health. Bobby's accident is just one example of how alcohol makes people do stupid things sometimes, which can result in loss of health, destruction of property, family devastation, permanent brain damage, or even death.

*For the drunkard and the glutton will come to poverty, and drowsiness will clothe **a man** with rags.*
(Proverbs 23:21)

In early adulthood, Tina's life was frequently touched by death and she began to think anyone she cared about would either leave her or die. Although all those losses were painful for her, the Lord now uses those experiences for Tina to help others going through loss. Tina can understand their pain, pray for them, and point them to the One who can give them the strength to face the grieving process head on. Often, it is in times of despair and sorrow we reach out to God.

*For our light affliction, which is but for a moment, is working for us a far more exceeding **and** eternal weight of glory, while we do not look at the things which are seen, but at the things which are not seen. For the things which are seen **are** temporary, but the things which **are** not seen are eternal.*
(2 Corinthians 4:17-18)

"These things I have spoken to you,
that in Me you may have peace.
In the world you will have tribulation;
but be of good cheer, I have overcome the world."
(John 16:33)

Our soul waits for the LORD;
He is our help and our shield.
For our heart shall rejoice in Him,
Because we have trusted in His holy name.
Let Your mercy, O LORD, be upon us,
Just as we hope in You.
(Psalm 33:20-22)

Are there SCARLET threads in your tapestry? [168]

_____
_____
_____
_____
_____
_____
_____
_____
_____
_____
_____
_____
_____
_____
_____
_____
_____
_____
_____

*We then who are strong ought to bear with the
scruples of the weak, and not to please ourselves.
Let each of us please **his** neighbor for **his** good,
leading to edification. For even Christ did not please
Himself; but as it is written, "The reproaches of those
who reproached You fell on Me." For whatever things
were written before were written for our learning,
that we through the patience and comfort
of the Scriptures might have hope.*
(Romans 15:1-4)

**Jesus's SCARLET thread was death on the cross
to give us life. How can God use the SCARLET
threads in your life?** [169]

_____
_____
_____
_____
_____
_____
_____
_____
_____
_____
_____
_____
_____
_____
_____
_____
_____
_____
_____
_____

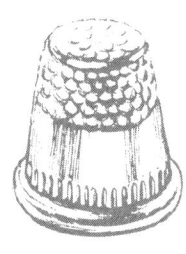

CHARTREUSE
Fight or Flight

Tina finally moved out of her parent's house in her early twenties. Her sister, Shawn, was the first to move out when she got married at eighteen. Then Tina's stepbrother Rick moved onto the boat with his grandmother, Ruth, as soon as he turned eighteen. Tina's younger brother, Brent, dropped out of high school to pursue professional fishing in Alaska and Mexico. Her older brother, Todd, left after an argument with their mom about staying out late resulted in her kicking him out. Tina's stepsister, Maggie, moved out when she was twenty.

Like Todd, Tina's moving out was prompted by an argument between her and her mom. Tina and Martha had some pretty bad arguments consisting of screaming profanities and hurtful words about how much they hated each other. With no model of what a loving relationship between mother and daughter was supposed to look like, Tina thought it was normal, in the heat of an argument, to hear her mother respond with the words, "I hate you too."

Sometimes relationships between mothers and daughters can be a bit tough, to say the least. Tina had always blamed her insecurities and self-doubt on her father leaving when she was so young. But, truth be told, as the Lord moved her to reflect on repeated difficulties in her life, she realized the relationship she had with her mother played a large part in her self-doubt. While Tina loves her mother dearly, it doesn't change the fact Martha did not know how to love Tina the way God created her to be loved. Instead, Tina's mother seemed to be in constant competition with her daughter. When Tina gained any positive recognition from others, her mother would often direct the attention back toward her own actions and achievements, or she would change the subject.

Tina's mom didn't have the best childhood. Martha was the third of four girls. Her father desperately wanted a boy. Martha's father was so convinced the baby was going to be the boy he had long awaited, he already had the name all picked out: Ray. Upon her birth, Martha's father was terribly disappointed to learn he had yet another girl. He named her Martha Ray.

Tina never met this grandfather. He died before she was born and Tina was probably better off not knowing him. He was an alcoholic who beat his wife, Tina's grandmother, when he got drunk. He would also beat his own daughters on occasion. In fact, Martha would often hide in the closet, frightened and in tears when she heard her father walk through the door after a long day at work. Martha never felt loved by her father. Martha was vulnerable and unprotected as a child and grew up with no model of what true unconditional love was supposed to look like.

Tina doesn't remember Martha often telling her she was proud of her for anything while she was growing up. So, Tina thought nothing she did or said was ever good enough or acceptable. The only time her mother seemed to like her was when Tina was dating someone her mom found acceptable. Thus began a long stream of relationships with men Tina thought her family would like enough to finally accept her. Yes, Tina actually thought if she could get a man to love her who her family admired, then her family—especially her mother—would love and accept her. Tina's yearning for acceptance played a large part in her decision to date Gage, a good-looking artist and aspiring screenwriter. And Nate, a three-time Emmy award-winning film editor; and Beau, the director of a prominent art gallery in Beverly Hills. None of these men knew Christ, and Tina had yet to allow the Lord to meet her intense need for love and acceptance.

In her early forties, Tina had surgery on her left foot. Her foot had been sore for some time, making it difficult to walk. Tina finally decided to do something about it and had a bunionectomy. Martha insisted Tina stay with them so she could care for her daughter after the surgery. Before being released from the hospital, the doctor explained just how bad the pain may be for the first few days. The surgery involved cutting the bone in two places, straightening it, and pinning it back together. A portion of the pin was left sticking out of a small incision on the top of Tina's foot for easy removal once the bone healed together properly. The surgeon instructed Martha to allow Tina to take one pain pill an hour if necessary to ease the pain, rather than every four hours as indicated on the label. Remember, Tina has a higher than normal pain threshold—she waited two days before seeing a doctor when she broke her wrist, and walked for nearly two hours on a broken foot. But following foot surgery, the pain Tina experienced was like nothing she'd ever felt before; it was excruciating!

"It felt like someone took a huge knitting needle, stuck it in a red-hot fire, and inserted the burning hot needle into the center of the bone in my foot," Tina recalled.

Unfortunately, even though the doctor instructed Martha to allow Tina to take the pain medication once per hour, Tina's mom refused to give her another pill before the four hours as instructed on the bottle. The pain was so intense Tina actually cried aloud in pain, waking her mother up, the first night. Storming into the guest room, Martha scolded Tina for waking her up, telling her it wasn't time for her to take another pain pill. Tina spent the rest of the night literally crying into her pillow and writhing in pain. Looking back, Tina realizes that her mother was probably acting out of fear.

A few years later, Tina was working through some of the childhood incidences that skewed her thinking regarding love and sex. She became aware that the sexual experimentation by her siblings wasn't healthy. It took Tina time to fully understand that how she was taught about sex and love didn't line up with what God's word says. She had always thought the kind of sexual immorality she experienced in her own family was normal, and didn't realize how damaging it had been for her until later.

Tina blamed herself for much of what happened, including the time Rick attempted to have sex with her before she even knew what sex was. A trusted pastor explained to Tina that what had happened to her as a child wasn't her fault. It is supposed to be the parent's responsibility to protect their children when they're young. Tina began to see herself differently, and realized God will always be there to protect her.

At the recommendation of the pastor, Tina was encouraged to speak to her parents, particularly her mother, about some of the things that happened to her as a child. Tina made an appointment for them both to see the counselor Martha had been seeing at the time. Sitting in the dimly lit room full of feminine decor and pillows, Tina began telling the Martha what had happened when she was a little girl; about the sexual experimentation that was going on—particularly as it related to what was done to her. It was difficult and painful for Tina to express. Martha didn't recognize there was anything wrong with what had happened to Tina.

Looking intently into Martha's eyes, the counselor elucidated how wrong it was and how vulnerable little Tina was without the proper protection from her parents. The words took a while to sink in for Martha, never feeling protected herself as a young child. Martha seemed to have accepted the truth that the sexual exploration attempted on Tina was not appropriate. For Tina's sake the counselor urged Martha to talk to Rick and explain that what he had done to Tina when she was young was wrong. Martha agreed, after a great deal of persuasion. Unfortunately, such a confrontation never took place. Quite the contrary as Martha and Larry took Rick out to dinner that very night, just hours after leaving the counselor's office. Once again, Tina felt as though she was the one who was looked down upon while Rick was being rewarded.

Tina is now aware her mom doesn't have the capability to love her the way God created her to be loved, but it still hurts sometimes. Tina thanks her heavenly Father that He loves her just the way she is, dents and all, so much so He sent His one and only Son to die for her. Tina loves her mom, and prays for her often. The Lord has recently allowed them some sweet times together, and Tina was able to assist both of her parents after surgery. She could never have been there for them had it not been for the love of Christ. The Lord continues to heal their relationship and Tina accepts that Martha loves her the only way she knows how.

No matter what our mom, dad, or anyone else for that matter, says to or about us, we can know God sees us as precious in His sight. He loves us just the way we are. When we fall short of perfection, God doesn't love us any less and there's nothing we can do to make Him love us any more than He already does; He proved it on the cross of Calvary.

Behold what manner of love the Father has bestowed on us, that we should be called children of God!
(1 John 3:1)

Have you been listening CHARTREUSE lies that you're unlovable? [170]

_____
_____
_____
_____
_____
_____
_____
_____
_____
_____
_____

*How precious **is** Your lovingkindness, O God!*
Therefore the children of men put their trust under
the shadow of Your wings. They are abundantly
satisfied with the fullness of Your house, And You
give them drink from the river of Your pleasures.
*For with You **is** the fountain of life;*
In Your light we see light.
(Psalm 36:7-9)

But God demonstrates His own love toward us,
in that while we were still sinners, Christ died for us.

(Romans 5:8)

What new CHARTREUSE threads of truth is God revealing about you right now? [171]

_____

_____

_____

_____

_____

_____

_____

_____

_____

_____

_____

_____

_____

_____

_____

_____

_____

_____

_____

_____

_____

_____

_____

_____

_____

_____

_____

_____

_____

_____

_____

_____

Who shall separate us from the love of Christ?
Shall *tribulation, or distress, or persecution, or*
famine, or nakedness, or peril, or sword? Yet in all
these things we are more than conquerors through
Him who loved us. For I am persuaded that neither
death nor life, nor angels nor principalities nor
powers, nor things present nor things to come, nor
height nor depth, nor any other created thing, shall
be able to separate us from the
love of God which is in Christ Jesus our Lord.
(Romans 8:35, 37–39)

How deep is the CHARTREUSE thread of God's love woven into your life tapestry? [172]

_____

_____

_____

_____

_____

_____

_____

_____

_____

_____

_____

_____

_____

_____

_____

_____

_____

_____

_____

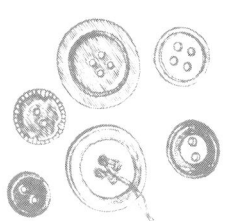

YELLOW
Traveling a World of No Boundaries

Tina took her first ride on an airplane with her friend Linda. Linda's aunt Valerie, a stewardess for American Airlines, gave them both tickets to fly from Los Angeles to San Diego where Valerie lived. Tina and Linda were both in grade school at the time so the trip was quite an adventure for the two young girls. Valerie took the girls to Sea World where Tina got to see, for the first time, the wonderfully entertaining dolphins, and watch the beautiful black and white killer whales perform with Sea World staff members. Tina sat mesmerized as she watched the enormous killer whales jump clear out of the water with a tiny human on its back. The three of them had a great, girly-girl, fun time together. Tina had never experienced anything like their girl time together, and felt very special to be included on this trip visiting Linda's beautiful Aunt Valerie.

Just out of high school, Tina had the privilege to go to Kauai with her sister Shawn and her husband, Kent, their daughter, Amy, her older brother, Todd, and her grandmother, Lilly, who came along to take care of Amy. This was the first time any of them had been to Hawaii, and they all fell in love with the island of Kauai. Kent and Todd were there mainly to surf, which they did a lot of. Tucked away all on its own, the house they rented was literally steps from the beach, below the lush tropical mountains of the north shore. So far north, in fact, they were smack dab in the middle of an area considered to be the wettest place on earth. When they drove up to the house at night, they would sit in the driveway with the motor running and the lights on, attempting to get some of the hundreds of frogs out of their way so when they walked to the front door they wouldn't have to step on too many (squish—yuck!).

Once inside, the family was welcomed by a plentiful array geckos and spiders. Tina didn't mind the geckos so much, but she could have done without the spiders. They were the biggest spiders she'd ever seen—huge! The huntsman spiders lurking on the walls every night were an ugly brown, with tremendously long legs, and measuring four to six inches across. Although non-venomous, they still gave Tina the heebie jeebies. Due to abundant rainfall, the island of Kauai is chock full of exotic flora and fauna. A sea of tropical green plants, trees, and ivy is constantly changing as God takes out His paintbrush and splashes the sea of green with pink, yellow, red, orange, and purple flowers. Kauai isn't called the Garden Isle for nothing; it's absolutely beautiful. Tina will never forget the wonderful times she had with her family, especially her sister Shawn, on that trip. Tina went to Hawaii three more times that year (Maui and Oahu), and twice again in recent years, (Kauai and Maui) but her first trip there is forever etched into her memory and heart. Kauai still is, and will always be, Tina's favorite island.

Most of the vacations Tina took in her early twenties consisted of going water-skiing and dirt bike riding with Shawn, Kent, and Todd. Tina fondly remembers many a night sitting around the campfire, singing together while Todd played guitar. Shawn and Tina became even closer as they shared some grand girl talk. Having such a good friendship with her older sister was something special to Tina. Shawn understood Tina; actually, they understood each other, sharing the same family background—they were best friends. Five or so years into Shawn's marriage to Kent, he started his own business, with Shawn's help, and they became fairly successful. After their second daughter, Tara, was born, Shawn and Kent bought dirt bikes, quads, and a huge motor home, and Tina would often join them camping and dirt bike riding in the desert. Though the girls may not have been strong riders like the boys, Shawn and Tina had a blast doing their fair share of riding. Little three-year-old Tara (a.k.a. T) would even ride on the quad with her mom on occasion and she loved it. Amusingly, little T fell asleep every time she rode between her mom's or dad's arms on the quad.

Kent, being a bit more creative than the other campers, would bring along a wooden dance floor to place near the campfire. They all had some pretty crazy times dancing at night in the middle of the desert, campfire roaring, music blaring, and various brands of alcohol pouring. Shawn and Tina both loved to cook and would create as gourmet of a meal as possible in the middle of the desert. The small kitchen of the motor home made cooking sometimes tricky, but also created some wonderful memories of Shawn and Tina breaking out in hysterical laughter as they ran into each other maneuvering their way around while cutting vegetables, grabbing for spices, or getting ingredients from the small refrigerator to the stove. Tina's niece, Amy, would sometimes help, while little Tara napped nearby.

When Shawn was pregnant with her third daughter, Kayla, they all spent a week on a rented houseboat and water-skiing on Lake Mead. Being six months pregnant, Shawn was a bit disappointed she couldn't water-ski, but she had fun driving the houseboat. Tina's beautiful little four-foot, eleven-inch tall sister, belly protruding with the baby, driving the huge houseboat was quite a sight. The thought of it still puts a smile on Tina's face.

Shawn and Tina took walks on the lakeshore with Amy and Tara, discussing ideas for meals, and exploring with the girls as they found interesting rocks, twigs, and other shore-side treasures. The sisters shared their most joyful memories, often stopping in their tracks and grabbing hold of their bellies, giggling like little girls, after Shawn's daughters would say something hilarious which reminded them of their own childhoods together. Tina didn't ski as much as she normally would have during that particular trip, but she got to spend a lot of time with Shawn and the girls, and has some beautiful memories as a result.

Tina had a few small jobs after high school. She worked at Hickory Farms during Christmas break (that was crazy!), Contempo Casuals, and Steve's Sporting Goods, but only when her mom helped get her a job at Mattel Toys did Tina feel she had a real job. Her first year at Mattel, Tina worked part-time as a statistical clerk which worked out well for her. She was able to finish two years of college by going to night school while working days. When Mattel started their electronics division, with the introduction of handheld electronic games, Tina applied for a full time position as an assistant in that department, and got the job. Tina had been working in the electronics division for just over a year when the division failed, and everyone was laid off. Tina was still young and, with her whole life ahead of her, the layoff didn't faze her. Those who were laid off from the electronics division were given top priority for openings in the toy division, so when a job became available in the samples/promotional services department requiring someone with artistic ability, Tina jumped at the chance. She presented her portfolio of artwork during the interview and, lo and behold, she got the job. Having someone outside the family recognize Tina for her artistic ability was affirming to her. Working in the promotional services department, Tina was involved in commercial shoots, trade shows, and advertising—anything and everything dealing with product promotion—and she began traveling extensively. Her first business trip with Mattel was to the New York Toy Fair. As Tina gained more and more recognition for her creativity and visionary thinking, Mattel began sending her to nearly every trade show. She traveled to several places: Michigan, Arizona;, New York, Puerto Rico, Mexico, Chile, Canada, Monaco, England and many others.

Before Tina was hired in the samples and promotional services department, Mattel had been simply displaying new toys on blocks covered with material and a plain back-drop with, perhaps, a few themed props for their sales presentations. Tina created an entirely new look and concept for every new toy line. She came up with the idea of using photographs in the background depicting a toy's theme. For example, for Bathtime Barbie, Tina designed a backdrop using a photograph of a woman's legs coming out of a bathtub of bubbles. Mattel loved the new looks, how the displays helped highlight the toy's theme better, and gave new product presentations more excitement and pop. Because she had designed the themes, Tina was also given the responsibility of organizing and directing photo shoots for the new product presentation backgrounds. And getting to design window displays in New York for the Toy Fair wasn't too shabby, either. Tina was able to be creative at Mattel. She even had the privilege of painting toy-themed murals on huge blank walls for some of the toy shows.

Tina had quite a time for a young girl in her mid twenties. She would often take advantage of the business travel by vacationing nearby wherever she had been sent to work on a trade show or commercial shoot. One year, Tina was sent to both Puerto Rico and Chile to work back-to-back trade shows. Being young and full of adventure Tina decided, four days prior to leaving, to vacation for a week in Rio de Janeiro, Brazil before returning to The States. She was warned by many people on the flight to Brazil to not go out by herself at night, not carry cash, not wear jewelry in public, and the list goes on. After checking into her hotel, Tina looked out her hotel room window and saw a raggedy old one-man shack, a graffiti-laden brick wall, and a trash-filled dirt alley. Such a depressing view was not really what she was looking for on vacation, so Tina decided to look for another hotel. Her first full day in Brazil, she switched hotels then spent a few hours on the beach, but the heat was unbearable, even for "never enough beach time" Tina. Early that evening, Tina took a walk on the boardwalk where the street peddlers were enthusiastically selling their wares. When the sun set, Tina realized she was out at night by herself. The peddlers, who she had been warned to stay away from, turned out to be some of the nicest people Tina met during her trip. They looked out for her, and even warned Tina when she did something foolish, like take large amounts of cash out of her wallet where it was visible for all to see. Tina enjoyed shopping on the boardwalk—the intricately handmade jewelry, arts, crafts, and gift items were beautiful, and the songs sung in Portuguese were exotically melodic.

For the next few days, Tina did what tourists do, which was unlike her. She visited Corcovado, the mountain peak with the famous statue of Jesus. Corcovado means "hunchback" in Portuguese. The view was breathtaking, and Tina took some wonderful pictures. Although she was not walking with Christ at the time, Tina sensed a great peace as she stood in wonderment and awe looking up at the amazing, enormous statue of Jesus.

Day three of her trip to Brazil, Tina joined a group of tourists for a lunch cruise and snorkeling. When they arrived at the beach where lunch was scheduled, Tina decided to stay on the boat and hang out with the crew rather than follow the other tourists and tour guide. Another boat with friends and family of the crew pulled alongside the tour boat, with music blaring, meat barbecuing, and kids ready for fun. Tina played with the children, jumping off the boat into the water; they all loved Tina and spoke to her in Portuguese as though she understood their every word. Tina didn't understand a word but they had a common bond of plain old fun. When the tour group returned, the guide yelled at the crew and Tina, suggesting that Tina should not have associated with the people from the other boat, since they were "strangers." She insinuated that Tina had put herself in a dangerous situation. Spending time with those strangers was the highlight of her trip; one Tina will never forget, and wouldn't change for the world. Tina had a great time, especially with the kids!

Do not forget to entertain strangers,
*for by so **doing** some have*
unwittingly entertained angels.
(Hebrews 13:2)

The fifth day of her trip to Brazil, Tina made her usual stop in the lobby to exchange traveler's checks for cash for the day. But there was a problem and they couldn't perform the transaction. The next morning, Tina checked at the front desk again but they were still unable to give her cash. So, beach for the weekend it was. The weather was hot, Hot, HOT—over 105 degrees Fahrenheit—so even sun-loving Tina had a difficult time hanging out on the beach all day. Jumping in the ocean didn't even cool her down. Tina couldn't wait until Monday so she could get the cash she needed to do some-thing different, something adventurous and fun. First thing Monday morning Tina was at the front desk again, only to learn they were still unable to cash her traveler's checks. She asked the hotel manager why they couldn't and he told her a big robbery at the bank was causing the problems. Skeptical of the story, Tina decided to call and check with the bank herself. They told her there had been no robbery, and there should be no problem cashing her traveler's checks. The hotel manager was upset that Tina had contacted the bank herself and still refused to exchange the traveler's checks for cash. Tina was shocked she was being treated in such a manner at such a high-end, large hotel.

All the banks now closed due to a country-wide bank strike, Tina still had no cash. She was frustrated and was ready to go home. Tina had no idea how she was supposed to even check out of the hotel since they weren't accepting her traveler's checks; she had no other means of payment. With some fear and trepidation, Tina asked the hotel manager for help. He instructed a cab driver to take Tina somewhere to cash her travelers checks. As they drove down narrow, trash-lined alleys, Tina's fear grew as the area seemed to be more and more destitute at each and every turn. The cab came to a stop in front of a small, run-down building and the driver instructed Tina to go in. Still frightened, Tina did as she was instructed and, thankfully, the rough-looking gentleman inside exchanged her traveler's checks for U.S. dollars.

Even though Tina hadn't seen much of Brazil, she was ready to go home. She paid the hotel bill in cash—U.S. dollars—checked out, and headed for the airport. Tina made it home safe and sound, but she wondered what would have happened if she had not been able to get the cash demanded by the hotel manager—the U.S. dollars they so desperately wanted.

God certainly protected Tina. Not only was she able to pay her hotel bill and leave, she was not assaulted or robbed by the street people, or kidnapped by the people she swam with during the lunch cruise.

> The LORD will protect you from all harm; He will protect your life. The LORD will protect your coming and going both now and forever.   (Psalm 121:7-8, HCSB)

One of Tina's friends from Mattel, Holly, often joined Tina on little adventures during their many travels for the company. The biggest Mattel trade show each year was held in the small country of Monaco on the French Riviera. Between the Mattel employees, buyers, and guests, they nearly took over the entire country. One particular trip to Monaco, Tina and Holly decided to take a train into San Remo, Italy instead of attending the big Mattel gala. They headed out at the crack of dawn, carrying only their passports, train tickets, and some cash. The beautiful, tall, redheaded Holly and short, little, blonde Tina got a lot of attention among the sea of dark Italians. They walked around window shopping, then went to have lunch when the shops began to close. The girls wondered why all but the restaurants were closing and learned from their waiter that the entire city closes down each day for pausa pranzo (lunch break). The only places open for the next four hours would be restaurants. So Tina and Holly had a leisurely lunch and consumed more than their fair share of Italian wine. They were pretty darn tipsy before the sun even set. As they left the restaurant at the end of pausa pranzo, people started pouring out of the woodwork.

The two girls enjoyed all the attention they were getting from Italian men, and had an increasing number of men following them. When four of the men offered to show Tina and Holly around town, the girls both agreed to allow the men to join them on their little adventure. Later that evening they all went to a small café for dinner. After dinner, they had been walking for just a little while when Tina suddenly realized she didn't have her passport, money, or train ticket. Tina was sure she had left them at the café, so she ran back to pick up those important items. Tina rushed to the table where they had been seated, but there was nothing there. Tina asked the café manager if they had found her passport, but was told they hadn't.

When Tina turned to look for Holly, thinking she and the four Italian men had been right behind her, Tina was shocked to find she was all alone. Tina ran back to where she had left the group, only to find them all gone. Gone? What? Holly was nowhere to be found, and Tina was now alone in Italy, with no passport, no money, and no train ticket. Tina scoured the small college town trying to find the group, but to no avail, so she returned to the café hoping Holly would at least come looking for her. Thirty minutes passed, then forty, then fifty, then an hour. Now sobering up, Tina really began to worry, feeling terrible about leaving Holly alone with strangers. Two hours passed, going on three; Tina was stuck in Italy by herself, with no way back to Monaco.

Tina asked the café manager once again, "Are you sure you didn't find my passport on the table? I'm sure I left it here." She hoped perhaps they would empathize with her enough to be honest. Apparently, the café manager had called the police and they pulled up at Tina's most distraught moment. The police tried to question Tina in broken English, but they couldn't communicate at all with each other. By this time, all Tina cared about was finding Holly. Tina was worried about her, and she managed to get the point across to the Italian police. The police drove Tina around the city to look for Holly among the crowds. At one point, Tina thought she saw Holly and asked the police to stop, jumping out of the police car before it had even come to a complete stop. With an Italian police officer running after her, rifle in hand, Tina ran up to the girl she thought was Holly only to learn, upon her turning around, it wasn't. The police then drove Tina to the train station, but Holly wasn't there, either, and the last train had already departed. So the policemen took Tina back to the police station, what else could they do with her at this point? Tina had no way back to Monaco, no passport, no ID, and no money. The chief officer attempted to reach someone from Mattel by calling the hotel in Monaco, but was unable because they were all at the opening night gala.

Tina had never smoked a day in her life, but joined the Italian officers in smoking cigarettes while they tried to comfort her, and decide what to do. Finally, nearing midnight they opted to simply put Tina in a cab and send her back to Monaco, in hopes someone from Mattel would be there to pay the cab driver. The timing was perfect! As the cab pulled up to the hotel, the gala was just ending when Tina's boss walked out just in time to pay the cab driver. Tina filled in her boss on the events of the night, and they voiced their concerns about Holly to the hotel manager, convincing him to let them into Holly's room to check if she was, by some chance, there. Sure enough, there was Holly, sleeping safe and sound in a nice, warm hotel bed. Tina was furious! She had been worried sick about her friend, but had, in fact, been abandoned by Holly in Italy without a way back. Drinking too much does this to you—it takes you out of your right mind, to do and say things you would never do or say in your right mind. There's good reason why God says "*And do not be drunk with wine, in which is dissipation;*" (*Ephesians 5:18*).

Holly showed up at the exhibit gallery in the morning none the worse for wear. Without apology, she told Tina she decided to take the train back and thought Tina had done the same. Holly never did explain where she had disappeared to with the men or why they didn't follow Tina back to the café.

Tina filed a police report in Monaco regarding her lost passport, and the following day she and a co-worker took a train to the American Embassy in Marseille to get Tina a new passport. Upon their return to the hotel, Tina was handed an envelope a police officer had left at the front desk. It was her passport. On the cover of her passport was a round indent, left by the end of a chair leg—the same kind of chair Tina had sat on in the café where they had dinner the night before. The same café where Tina was sure she had left her items.

About three years into her promotional services job at Mattel, Tina was getting really burned out with all the travel. Shawn just had her third child and divorced her husband, Kent, and she and Tina were starting to spend a lot more time together.

One summer night Shawn and Tina were dancing at a club in Redondo Beach, when they met three very handsome Navy men who were there for the summer. Tina and Shawn started hanging out with the Navy boys, meeting them at dance clubs and having fun at the beach. Soon, Tina was dating one of them, Cameron, a Navy corpsman (doctor). Just after they started dating she was sent by Mattel, for the second time, to Mexico City for a trade show. Tina really didn't want to go this time. Not only because of Cameron, but Mexico City was her least favorite location; it was filthy and, because of the horrible air pollution, the sky there is brown and dreary.

Nonetheless, Tina obediently left and off to Mexico City she went. One afternoon the electricity went out, as it often did, during a huge thunderstorm so they had to stop working and wait it out. Though the temperature was around 70 degrees Fahrenheit, because of the high altitude it began hailing. When they all ran outside to check out the hail and to take a picture with the boss, Tina slipped on a larger-than-normal marble stair hurting her foot. It hurt quite a bit, but with her higher than normal tolerance for pain, Tina just shrugged it off. While walking to dinner with a co-worker that night, the pain in Tina's foot started getting worse. Tina was able to make it back to the hotel after dinner, but walking on her foot had become unbearably painful. The next morning, Tina's foot was swollen and bruised. Tina showed her foot to one of the executives from Mattel Mexico, who sent her to the hospital for an x-ray, though Tina's boss didn't think it was necessary. Tina's foot was broken; yes, broken! The doctors at the hospital in Mexico City wrapped it in a poorly constructed plaster cast. When Tina returned to the office her boss exclaimed, "All that for a broken toe?" Tina felt bad she had injured herself. Working a trade show for Mattel was much like being on a construction site, as custom-themed rooms for each new toy would be built. It was difficult for Tina to maneuver around all the paint buckets, wood piles, boxes, and ladders in a cast, which only lasted a day before falling to pieces. Tina went back to the hospital and requested a waterproof cast. Fiberglass casts were new at the time. The executives at Mattel Mexico encouraged Tina to call Human Resources at Mattel Corporate Headquarters, who decided it best for Tina to return home. Tina's boss wasn't very happy that he didn't have the final say. One requirement of Tina being sent home was she had to go straight from LAX to a company-appointed doctor. The fiberglass cast was actually causing Tina some pain at this point so they removed it, but not without complications. The doctors in California didn't believe Tina when she told them the saw was hurting and cutting her leg. Because they were used to having a thick padding buffer between the hard cast and human flesh, it never dawned on them this cast might be different, having been put on in a different country. As it turned out, the doctors in Mexico City neglected to use any padding whatsoever; this was why the cast had been causing so much pain. The U.S. doctors were surprised when they got the cast off and noticed the saw had, in fact, cut Tina's leg.

Tina's boss at Mattel used to flirt with her a lot. Most of the time she would just laugh at his comments, being young and naïve. Sometimes she even enjoyed it, feeling it gave her some sort of self-worth, which she had little of to begin with. But after four years, his demeaning comments and gestures really began to get to her, though she did nothing to stop his behavior. Tina didn't tell her boss that his behavior was unacceptable; she didn't know what a boundary was, let alone how to set one. His reaction to Tina's broken foot was the last straw for her, though. Tina began looking for another job and quit Mattel after being offered a job at Silver Reed, the company her brother, Todd, worked for at the time.

Tina's job at Silver Reed was advertising and trade show coordinator. Silver Reed, a Japanese owned company, was a manufacturer of typewriters. At the same time they were introducing a type of personal computer they were marketing to secretaries who were used to working with typewriters. Personal computers were just being introduced. Being the creative type, Tina was intimidated at the mere thought of using a computer, but she thrived. Not only did she have the creative sense necessary for advertising and PR, she excelled at learning anything technical in nature. Perhaps she got it from her biological father, the genius and engineer.

The first trade show Tina oversaw for Silver Reed caused quite a bit of anxiety for her boss, since she had never done this type of typical convention center trade show. He was relieved and impressed when he arrived in Las Vegas and everything was set up as planned. The hospitality, customer focused events, booth set up, and everything else went off without a hitch. Tina continued to travel while working at Silver Reed, but the trips were in the United States only and not half as long as the traveling Mattel required. With Mattel she was gone for three or more weeks at a time and, more often than not, was only home long enough to pay rent before leaving again.

The executives of Silver Reed eventually hired someone to oversee the marketing department. During one of her business trips to Chicago, Tina's new boss took her out and wined and dined her. After dinner he kissed Tina and told her he wanted her to be his girlfriend, but he was married! Tina felt uncomfortable but, once again, didn't know how to respond, so what did she do? She started looking for another job. Tina interviewed for a marketing coordinator job at a company close to home, and gladly accepted when she was offered the job. The company had created the position for Tina based on the answers she gave during her interview; the only stipulation Tina made in accepting their offer was there be little to no travel.

Boundary—what's a boundary? Tina didn't know how to say no, and would often throw her pearls before swine, only to have them trampled underfoot. Boundaries help us keep the good in and the bad out. Saying no to the bad is OK. So much of how Tina lived was based on her extreme desire and need for approval from men, rather than the approval of God. We are of great value to God and should live in that knowledge.

Do not give what is holy to the dogs; nor cast your pearls before swine, lest they trample them under their feet, and turn and tear you in pieces.
(Matthew 7:6)

*Walk in wisdom toward those **who** are outside, redeeming the time. **Let** your speech always **be** with grace, seasoned with salt, that you may know how you ought to answer each one.*
(Colossians 4:5-6)

Is God revealing some YELLOW threads of boundaries that He wants you to set? [173]

He who has begun a good work in you will complete it until the day of Jesus Christ; (Philippians 1:6)

What are some of the YELLOW adventures God has allowed you to experience? How is He strengthening you through them? [174]

_____
_____
_____
_____
_____
_____
_____
_____
_____
_____
_____
_____
_____
_____
_____
_____
_____
_____
_____
_____
_____
_____
_____
_____
_____

BLACK
The Adventure of Adversity

Tina's stepgrandma, Ruth, was diagnosed with Parkinson's disease just a few years after her husband, Barry, died. Ruth was active, and able to fend for herself for several years following the diagnosis, but her mind and body slowly deteriorated. Watching such a vibrant woman fade was difficult for Tina. Ruth had continued living on *The Yankee*, but eventually could no longer get around, and living on a boat surrounded by water was dangerous, so she had to move to a nursing home where she would be watched and cared for. The decision to move her broke her son, Larry's, heart. Tina realized the severity of Ruth's failing health first one night when the family was out together for dinner. Ruth had an accident before she was able to make it to the restaurant's bathroom, and Tina helped Ruth clean up. Ruth was embarrassed, and kept apologizing. Tina felt very close to her at that moment, and was saddened by Ruth's weakness and shame. Eventually, Ruth deteriorated to the point she had to be hospitalized. Knowing she was nearing her last day on earth, Tina's family visited Ruth at the hospital often. The night Ruth died, Larry, Rick, and Tina were there with her. It was a sad day. It was hard for Tina to see her step-father cry out as he watched his mother gasp her last breath. Gazing out the hospital room window after her passing, Tina saw a shooting star. A true gift from God—you don't see a shooting star only twenty miles south of Los Angeles, every day! Ruth was cremated and her ashes scattered at sea by her family, off *The Yankee*. At the time, Tina was not walking with the Lord, and didn't give any thought to where she would go when she died.

A few years after Ruth passed away, Tina's grandma Lilly died. Lilly had been sick with congestive heart failure, and was living with her daughter, Pam, so she could be taken care of. Martha spent a lot of time at her sister's house, helping take care of her ailing mother. Martha relished the time she was able to spend with her mother. Throughout her childhood, Martha had never heard the words "I love you," come out of Lilly's mouth. Martha spent every minute she could taking care of her mother, hoping against all hope that she would hear her Lilly finally say the words "I love you" to her before she died. Sadly, that never happened; Martha never once heard the words "I love you" come out of her mother's mouth. Now the family's token Christian, they family asked Tina to say something at her grandma's memorial service. She was honored to do so. It gave Tina an opportunity to speak about how Jesus is the only One who could fill the void left in their hearts by the loss of Lilly.

Early in their marriage, Shawn and Kent started their own business, and became very successful. The marriage didn't survive, but the company they formed did, and Shawn didn't have to work after their divorce. She and Tina spent a lot of time together, dancing three nights a week and going dirt bike riding. They would pack up their dirt bikes, riding gear, and all the necessary tools into Shawn's motorcycle trailer and head out to the desert to ride. Three nights a week, Shawn and Tina went to a restaurant in Long Beach, on the nights the bar area turned into a punk club called the Gargoyle Lounge. Shawn and Tina met a lot of nice people there, many of whom—including the Mohawk-sporting DJ—were Christians. Influenced by the people they were hanging out with, both Shawn and Tina stopped drinking alcohol when they went out. Instead, they drank Diet Coke and smoked clove cigarettes like all the other Gargoyle Lounge regulars. How in the world did Tina manage to work an eight-hour day after dancing all night long, getting in after 3:00 a.m. every Tuesday, Thursday, and Sunday? Oh, the fountain of youth.

After her divorce, Shawn moved into a small house on the beach in Hermosa. After Shawn bought the motorcycle trailer, she and Tina started going dirt bike riding together more and more. Shawn was a much better rider than Tina, but eventually Tina bought a faster bike. One day, while out riding with Christian Gargoyle DJ Ray, and having had a not-so-hearty breakfast of diet soda, Tina started feeling dizzy after the first hill climb. It was an extremely hot day, and one of the first times she had ridden her brand-new motorcycle. She stopped and took off her helmet to get some air. Shawn and Ray thought Tina was simply being a wimp. Not wanting to put a damper on the day's ride, Tina put her helmet back on and off they went. After about thirty minutes of riding, Tina was feeling nauseous and light headed. She stopped again, turned off her bike, took her helmet off, then laid down on the ground with the bike beside her, urging Shawn and Ray to go on without her. Of course they wouldn't, insisting they all make their way back to base camp together. The ride back was extremely difficult for Tina, feeling so ill, but Shawn and Ray rode behind her. Ray had to take Tina's bike down the last hill, and she took her helmet off, slowly walking the rest of the way. Tina had heat stroke. Having only a diet soda for breakfast before a long ride on a hot day certainly didn't help matters. Even though it wasn't the best riding day, it is a fond memory for Tina because she was with Shawn and they had fun joking and eating lunch once safely back at base with the other riders.

Now living on her own, Shawn made a point of painting nearly every day. Her paintings were full of emotion—mostly dark, dramatic, and sometimes depressing. Tina learned a lot from Shawn's artistic creativity and style, and Shawn's influence shows in some of Tina's paintings today. Tina enjoyed her deep discussions with Shawn about life, God, and church, but, more often than not, they talked about their insecurities and men. Neither Tina nor Shawn were going to church or walking in obedience back then, but Tina will never forget the influence of a U2 concert at the

Los Angeles Sports Arena during their Joshua Tree tour. Tina managed to get tickets in the eighth row, center, for a mere $200 each. The sisters had heard rumors about the members of U2 being Christian. Shawn was touched by their songs, so the post-concert conversation between she and Tina consisted of discussions about God, Jesus, the church, and where each of them were in life. Both the girls had questions deep down, but that didn't keep them from the sinful lifestyle they were living. With sex, drugs and rock 'n' roll, Tina and Shawn were trying to fill a void only God can fill.

Shawn met her second husband, Parker, when she was out dancing one night without Tina. Shawn told Tina she had met a man she was extremely attracted to. Shawn and Parker started dating, and Tina would often go out with Shawn and Parker, and one of Parker's friends, Ron. Shawn and Parker were dating exclusively when Shawn told Tina he and Ron both did drugs. Shawn had been ashamed to tell Tina at first, but drug use was somewhat cool at the time, because it seemed all the rock stars did drugs. Tina began dating Ron, and they all began doing drugs together.

Parker eventually moved in with Shawn and, less than a year into their relationship, they got married. Shawn continued to enjoy life after marrying Parker, only now her enjoyment included using drugs with Parker. About six months into their marriage, they moved to Costa Mesa and Tina was no longer included in their fun. Shawn began intentionally separating her life from Tina's in an attempt to protect Tina from the devastating effects of the couple's drug use. Within a year of being married, Shawn shared with Tina and a few of her close friends from the Gargoyle Lounge that she was trying to stop using drugs, but it was difficult since Parker was still using in front of her. One night, after a family bowling outing, Tina and Shawn were walking through the parking lot when Shawn said Parker was afraid she was going to leave him, and, indeed, she was seriously working toward leaving him in an attempt to get her life back on track and drug free.

A few weeks later, Tina's boyfriend at the time, Walker, was staying with her after a night out dancing, when **Tina got the worst phone call of her life.** At around three in the morning, the phone rang. Tina's brother, Todd, was on the line and asked Tina, "Were you with Shawn tonight?" He was obviously upset. Walker and Tina hadn't seen Shawn that night. Todd then demanded Tina meet him at their parents' house in Torrance even though her parents were staying on *The Yankee* at the time. The drive over seemed to take forever in Tina's state of heightened anxiety. Tina tried rationalizing the call, telling Walker everything must be OK, since Todd hadn't said otherwise. But, deep down inside, Tina knew something was terribly wrong. But never, in a million years, would Tina have imagined the words she was about to hear. Todd wasn't there yet when Walker and Tina arrived at her parents' house. When Tina saw Todd's car pull up into the driveway, she opened the front door and stood waiting for him. Todd walked up the front walkway and, standing in front of Tina exclaimed, "Shawn's dead." Tina screamed, "NO. NO! NO!!" and ran down the front walkway in tears. Tina stopped helplessly, losing control, she crouched down sobbing with her head in her hands. Tina felt a deep sense of utter helplessness. Someone she loved more than anyone else in the world was gone due to a drug overdose, and there was nothing Tina could do about it. Shawn understood Tina better than anyone else in this world.

The following day, all of Shawn's siblings met at the house in Torrance before driving down to the boat to break the news to their parents. Martha was initially excited to see them all, unaware of why they were there. When Todd told her about Shawn she cried out, "My baby, no, not my baby!" At one point, Todd said, "I didn't even know my own sister!" But Tina knew her sister, better than anyone and she felt very alone, as if no one else in the family could understand her pain.

Because Shawn was married, Parker was the only one who had rights to Shawn's body. He had an open casket viewing, which Shawn would have never wanted. Tina didn't go to the viewing, but did attend the memorial service Parker had the following day. Few people attended, and the man who spoke about Shawn sounded as though he was talking about someone else altogether. Those people really didn't know Shawn at all, and only spoke of the Shawn they knew during the year she was married to Parker. Shawn had lived in utter darkness with Parker and his crazy friends, who built caskets to sleep in, one of which was the most prominent piece of furniture in their living room. Todd and Walker accompanied Tina to Parker's memorial for Shawn. Afterward, Parker invited them to attend the sprinkling of her ashes at sea, but they were all so disgusted by the words spoken about a woman no one seemed to know, they declined. Tina's entire family blamed Parker for Shawn's death, since he had introduced her to drugs.

Shawn's family had their own memorial service to celebrate the life of the real Shawn. The service took place at Malaga Cove, a beautiful cove in Palos Verdes where Shawn used to go surfing with Todd. Larry played a melodically emotional rendition of "Amazing Grace" on his saxophone, standing at the ocean's edge, while Todd slowly paddled out on his surfboard with the beautifully colorful array of flowers everyone brought, and gracefully placed them into the sea. Tina tearfully watched the flowers drift away into the distance.

Tina misses Shawn more than anyone she's lost. No one knew her like Shawn did. No one understood Tina like Shawn did. No one loved her as unconditionally as Shawn did. Tina hopes and prays she gets to see her beautiful sister when the Lord takes her home. Shawn went through confirmation class at Seaside Community Church[8] when she was in junior high, but there's really no way to know if Shawn ever submitted her life to, and put her faith in, Jesus as her Lord and Savior. Tina certainly would like to believe she did. But, even though Tina was intermittently attending church at Hope Chapel[9] in Hermosa Beach and Calvary Chapel South Bay[10], neither she nor Shawn were truly walking with the Lord while Shawn was alive. All Tina can do is lay it before the Lord, and trust He will give her a chance to see Shawn again if it's His will. This spurs Tina on with a greater desire to share the gospel with others, especially her loved ones. Tina recognizes, however, that she is not the one responsible for the salvation of others; only God is. Tina realizes she cannot pick and choose who goes to heaven and who doesn't, as much as it grieves her sometimes. Tina knows she needs to trust in the One who will wipe away every tear from our eyes, remove our sorrow, and give us peace in the end.

After Shawn's death Tina's family didn't want her talking to Parker, in spite of the fact that he had all of Shawn's belongings. Todd and Kent were supposed to make arrangements with Parker to get Shawn's piano, her artwork, and some of her personal belongings, but they never seemed to be able to get it together. So, without letting anyone in her family know, Tina went and visited Parker one day and got a few of Shawn's paintings, but that's it. There's so much more of her they never got back from him; mainly her soul.

> *Therefore you now have sorrow;*
> *but I will see you again*
> *and your heart will rejoice,*
> *and your joy no one will take from you.*
> *(John 16:22)*

Tina's stepsister, Maggie, wasn't treated very well by her peers growing up because she had a learning disability. But she did eventually meet a man, Ben, who seemed to love her. Maggie moved to Florida with Ben and they had a daughter together. Now in her mid-thirties, Tina was attending a trade show in Orlando and she took advantage of the opportunity meeting Walker who happened to be in Florida at the same time. He worked for Hughes Aircraft and was in Florida for a shuttle launch. They took a little mini-vacation to visit

Maggie and her family. Tina was excited to see Maggie; she hadn't seen her in years. Ben seemed very controlling, not letting Maggie or their daughter, Mary, out of his sight for a second. Tina's visit was near Christmas, and Maggie was decorating their apartment. Maggie was so proud of her home and family. She eagerly showed Tina a Christmas tree topper they had just purchased—an angel. Wanting to make Maggie feel good, Tina complimented her for picking out such a beautiful tree topper. Just when Maggie and Mary were ready to place the angel on top of the tree, Ben insisted that Maggie give the cherished tree topper to Tina. Tina told Ben it wasn't necessary for Maggie to give her the precious angel, but he absolutely insisted. Tina felt sorry for Maggie as she slowly handed the precious angel to her.

Maggie had been ill with Crohn's disease for some time and eventually had to have surgery. The surgery went fine and she was released from the hospital, but two weeks later she died of unexplained heart failure. Ben didn't inform the family of any funeral or memorial services for Maggie, and they don't even know where she is buried. Back home in California, Tina's family had no memorial service for Maggie like they had for Shawn.

Tina lost both of her sisters within a year and a half of each other.

> *And God will wipe away every tear from their eyes; there shall be no more death, nor sorrow, nor crying. There shall be no more pain, for the former things have passed away. (Revelation 21:4)*

Linda, a friend of Tina's since elementary school, asked Tina to be in her wedding. Tina was excited that Linda was getting married and eager to participate in her friend's wedding. But the day before the rehearsal dinner, Tina was robbed at gunpoint in front of her home in Redondo Beach. Tina didn't live in a bad area, and never thought a criminal would be out searching for his next victim at 7:30

in the morning, when people were beginning their day and driving to work. Tina's weekday morning routine included checking her mail. Tina's apartment was at the back of the complex, and the mailboxes were in the front. So, on her way to work, Tina would drive up the driveway, pull the key out of the ignition, unlock her mailbox, get her mail, put the key back in the ignition and be on her merry way.

On this morning, she had put her camera case with camera, lenses, etc., and her purse in the back of her hatchback, because she planned to shoot some product photos for work. When she drove up the driveway, Tina noticed a man on the opposite side of the street wearing blue jeans, a black turtleneck, black shoes, and a black beanie, which she thought strange. When Tina made eye contact with the man, she was frightened. She was alone in her car and, because her keys were still in the mailbox, had no way to escape. The the man looked away and continued walking, easing Tina's fear. Her sense of relief didn't last long, though, as the man scanned the street and, seeing there were no other people around, began making his way toward her. Still in her car, Tina started rolling up her car window when the man ran toward her, stuck a gun to her head, and demanded her purse.

Tina instinctively put her hands in the air, exclaiming, "It's in the back, it's in the back." He ordered Tina to open the hatchback. While he grabbed things out of the car, Tina kept her hands in the air, fearing he would shoot her because she had looked him straight in the eyes. A few minutes passed when Tina saw him running off with her camera case and purse. Her first thought was to drive after him, but her keys weren't in the ignition, so she left the car door wide open and ran back to her apartment to call 911. After what felt like an eternity, a police officer finally showed up at her doorstep. The officer had Tina fill out a police report and asked her if she had record of the serial numbers for her camera equipment. "No, I don't." Tina responded, at which time the officer advised her that the chances were slim to none that her items would ever be recovered. Tina was distraught that one of her primary creative outlets—her camera—was stolen from her.

A few days after the robbery, Tina called the police department to follow up on her case. Though they had nothing satisfying to report, the police did provide Tina with information about victims' assistance, a program developed to assist victims of violent crimes. Tina found the fact that the program is funded through inmate jobs and criminal fines paid to be the most gratifying part of the program for her. She also got the name of a counselor who treated victims of violent crimes. Until the robbery, Tina had been an adventurous woman who walked with confidence, but after the robbery she walked fearfully in public. Tina was upset to now need pointers from a counselor on how to walk with a look of confidence. What bothered Tina most about the robbery wasn't the loss of her camera, purse, money, or even the beautiful brooch she had bought in London; it was the fact that what had happened had robbed her of her independence. At the same time, though, she wondered what happened to make someone want to commit such a crime, and Tina felt sorry for the man.

Moving on with her life, Tina did participate as a bridesmaid in Linda and Joel's wedding. It was a beautiful celebration of the love they had for one another. Tina was happy to be standing next to the beautiful bride as she spoke her wedding vows. Linda finally had her dream life, a husband who loved her, a new house, a brand-new baby girl, and a stepson she loved, but that would all be ripped out from under her in the blink of an eye.

On Mother's Day of 1992, Tina's family was at her place for dinner when she received a phone call from Linda's brother, Dante. He told Tina Linda's husband Joel had been shot and killed, and Linda had also been shot and was in intensive care.

Linda and Joel had just had their first baby—a beautiful girl they named Brittany—one month before, and had also just celebrated their one-year wedding anniversary. A young man, high on drugs broke into to their home, sexually assaulted Linda, and then shot her and her husband Joel. Joel died instantly but Linda was still alive. As the intruder ransacked the house, Linda pretended she was dead. From listening to the television, she figured about two hours had passed. When she didn't hear any more movement in the house, Linda made her way to the neighbors where she pounded on the door with what strength she could muster. They called 911, and Linda was rushed to the hospital.

Once in the emergency operating room, the doctors removed the bullet which had ricocheted in and through her arm, into her chest, and down through her liver and other internal organs. It was a miracle that Linda was still alive.

A few days later, Linda's family said Tina could visit her in the hospital. Linda was still in ICU but, even though Tina wasn't family, they let her in. Tina remembers walking past the police officer sitting outside the hospital room door, which made it all so real. They were there to protect her friend from the man whose actions forever changed her life. Tina was overcome with emotion when she saw Linda lying there, covered in bandages, arms full of tubes, and machines lit up and beeping, monitoring her vital signs. As Tina approached her bedside, Linda looked up and said, "I thought these kinds of things only happened to you." Linda then asked her dad to leave the room so the women could be alone and cry.

The intruder was found and arrested some days later. Things like this never happened back then in sunny Torrance, and the press had a field day. The doctors allowed Linda to leave the hospital to attend Joel's funeral. It was a sad day for all who knew the fun-loving couple.

After Linda was released from the hospital she expressed a desire to make a video showing what her life was like before the crime was committed compared to what her life was like now, after the murder of her husband. Tina was working at LVM at the time and had befriended a videographer named Trent who she hired to shoot corporate videos. Tina introduced Trent to Linda and he gladly agreed to put together a video for her. The video showed clips of

Linda and Joel's wedding, Brittney's birth and the simple joy and laughter they shared together as family. Linda took Trent to the cemetery where they shot video of Linda holding baby Brittney as she tearfully shared how empty her life was without Joel and how Brittney would never know her father. This video would later play a significant role in the trial.

All of these BLACK threads were woven into Tina's tapestry within a two year period. Those were the darkest, most difficult, two years of Tina's life.

> *Likewise the Spirit also helps in our weaknesses. For we do not know what we should pray for as we ought, but the Spirit Himself makes intercession for us with groanings which cannot be uttered.*
> *(Romans 8:26)*

As a result of the Christian concert she attended in high school, Tina still prayed nearly every day, and read the Bible every once in a while, although she didn't quite understand it. She had never doubted the reality of Jesus and who He was until after those two BLACK years. Tina began spending more time partying, drinking with Trent and his friends, many of whom were famous rock stars who didn't believe in God at all. With all her loss and pain, Tina had allowed the company she was keeping to influence what she believed, and she began to doubt the truth of God, Jesus, and the validity of the Bible. She stopped praying, and would have nothing to do with the Bible or Christians.

*In this you greatly rejoice, though now for a little while, if need be, you have been grieved by various trials, that the genuineness of your faith, **being** much more precious than gold that perishes, though it is tested by fire, may be found to praise, honor, and glory at the revelation of Jesus Christ, whom having not seen you love. Though now you do not see **Him**, yet believing, you rejoice with joy inexpressible and full of glory, receiving the end of your faith— the salvation of **your** souls. (1 Peter 1:6-9)*

Are you grieving in the midst of BLACK trial right now? Can you see Jesus through the tears? [175/176]

_____

_____

_____

_____

_____

_____

_____

_____

_____

_____

_____

_____

_____

_____

_____

_____

_____

_____

_____

Although Tina didn't recognize it at the time, she can now look back on this dark time in her life—especially the loss of her sister and the robbery at gunpoint—and see how the Lord had prepared her to be there for Linda. Unfortunately, we live in a fallen world full of sinners. Because of this, we experience pain and suffering. But, rest assured, God can use the difficult times you experience in life to allow you to help others going through trials and difficulty.

Read *2 Corinthians 1:3-7;* how might the Lord use the BLACK threads in your tapestry to help encourage and comfort others? [177]

TAN
Naked and Alone

Lens Vision Machinery (LVM) is a private, family owned business. The owner was Frank. His oldest son, Kevin, was in charge of operations; his younger son, Dan, worked in production on occasion; his oldest daughter, Janet, was an interior designer who would periodically do some office design; and his youngest daughter, Karen, was a photographer who would photograph the large machines. Frank had a photography studio/showroom built for testing the machines, customer demonstration purposes, and product photography. As marketing coordinator, Tina's duties included directing photo shoots, product illustration, advertising, public relations, and the like.

Tina had only been working at LVM a short time when her boss, Jack, resigned when a new marketing director was hired, and Tina was promoted to replace Jack as marketing manager. Tina had her dream job with a private corner office, an assistant, and a marketing staff who worked under her. Though, on paper, Tina reported directly to Susie, the new marketing director, Tina received most of her direction from the owner, Frank. Tina was intrigued by stories of how Frank came up with the idea for the lens vision machine, and his intelligence impressed her. Tina enjoyed writing press releases introducing new machines and the technology behind them, designing product brochures, writing scripts, producing, and directing corporate videos, and everything to do with introducing new LVM products and promoting the company. Tina was a proud LVM employee, and passionate about her job.

After Jack left, Tina became close to Frank, and he would often come into her office just to talk. One day, Susie approached Tina and told her she should ask Frank for money to buy clothes for work. Tina would have never thought of doing such a thing, and considered the suggestion strange. But Susie was insistent and, since Tina was too chicken to do so, Susie asked Frank directly to give Tina money for clothes. The first time Frank gave Tina $200 cash, she used it to buy a couple of dresses for work. Frank became a father figure to Tina, someone she thought truly cared about her. The second time Frank was giving Tina money for clothes, Tina suggested that, since it was his money, he should go shopping with her to pick out the clothes himself. The LVM Christmas party was approaching and Tina needed something nice to wear. Frank took her to the mall and bought Tina two formal outfits—a beautiful blue dress and an intricately beaded black jumpsuit. Tina had never owned such elegant outfits before, and felt Frank was treating her like one of his own daughters.

Frank frequently came to Tina's office after hours, when everyone else was gone. At first, Tina thought it was simply because they could get more work done with no interruptions. Frank began talking to Tina about her family, her sister's death, her biological father, her mom, and other emotionally charged topics. Tina believed that Frank really cared about her. Tina often put herself down when it came to her looks, especially her body. She was obsessed with her weight, wanting to make sure she didn't look fat. Frank's compliments on how good her body looked made Tina feel accepted. But soon he began talking more frequently about her looks and her body, and Tina started to feel uncomfortable around him. As Frank's comments progressively became more intimate in nature, Tina began to dread him coming by her office, especially after hours.

Tina was home sick one day when she noticed someone lurking on her front porch. She was watching television when Frank peeked his head through her curtains, scaring Tina half to death. The townhouse Tina rented was owned by Frank's daughter, Janet, so he had keys to the security gate. Frank knocked on the sliding glass door. Her heart still pounding from fright, Tina reluctantly opened the door and asked Frank what he was doing there. He told Tina he had come by to make sure she was OK. Couldn't he have called to check on her? Tina found the visit rather creepy, but said nothing to him, or anyone else, about him coming over uninvited and unannounced. Internally avoiding reality, Tina talked herself out of acknowledging how wrong his actions were. She so desperately wanted a father figure who seemed proud of her, she didn't care what he did.

Tina went to the LVM Christmas party with Frank's youngest son, Dan, that year. Tina had a good time in spite of Dan alluding to the fact he really wanted to be there with Susie. Dan and Susie had been having an affair. Susie was married to a good man and they had a beautiful daughter together. Unfortunately neither kept her from having affairs with men she thought could help advance her career. In fact, Susie flat out told Tina she would do whatever it took to get to the top, no matter who she had to step on to get there.

After the Christmas party, Dan and Tina became closer, and had many conversations about his strong love for Susie, and his disappointment when she stopped talking to him. Susie was spending more and more time with Dan's father, Frank, the owner of the company. The less time Susie spent with Dan, the more obsessed about her Dan became. At one point, Dan's own father had him escorted off the LVM premises by the police. Susie told Tina Dan had become addicted to drugs, asking Tina questions about drug addiction, assuming she would know a lot since Tina's sister died of an overdose. Not long after, the inner turmoil and emotional pain got the best of Dan, and he shot himself to death in front of his parents. This was a devastating time for the entire LVM family.

Tina was socializing a lot with LVM employees and often had dinner parties at her house, where they would all drink. Slowly, one drink a week became two, two became three, three became four, and so on until Tina started drinking every single night. Tina reasoned away her excessive alcohol con- sumption—after all, she was simply having a glass of wine to relax after a hard day's work, just as so many others do.

Tina was working exorbitantly long hours and began seeing a counselor to help her deal with the stress. Frank had become exceedingly flirtatious with her which, added to Tina's stress. He started touching Tina's breasts in conjunction with discussions about her weight. Being raised without boundaries, Tina didn't know how to respond and would often giggle a nervous laugh and tell Frank to "stop it." Tina abhorred the thought of Frank coming into her office, especially after hours but Tina couldn't stop him; he was the owner of the company! She didn't want to loose her job. Tina never told anyone what Frank had been doing to her. Tina considered telling her counselor, especially after Frank had attempted to put his hand between her legs. Once again, Tina had just giggled nervously and told him to stop it, crossing her legs to keep him from touching her there.

Tina had been working on the company catalog for nearly two years. She worked long hours, with little sleep, in order to finish the project in time for an upcoming trade show. The catalog was finally going to print, when a top LVM sales manager pointed out an imperative change. Because Frank was at one of the LVM offices in Europe, Tina faxed the requested changes to him. Later in the day, Frank called Tina from Europe barking, "Why did you show the catalog to the sales manager? How dare you!" Absolutely exhausted, Tina started shaking, and actually broke down crying on the phone. Frank's voice changed as he responded by telling her, "Stop it, you know I love you, don't you?" Tina was angry he would treat her that way after she had worked so hard for him and his company! The Lord had begun to open her eyes that his treatment toward her was wrong.

Tina called her brother Todd later that day and explained what had happened and how hard she had been working. Todd insisted she come stay with him and his family, so she drove to his house and called in sick the following day. Todd and his wife were concerned about Tina, encouraging her not to return to work. Until the night before they had no idea how much stress Tina was under, or how Frank had been sexually harassing her for the past four years. When

Todd was at work a few days later, Tina opened up to his wife Summer and told her how Frank had been touching her. When Todd called later to check in, Summer told him there was more to Tina's situation than they originally thought. Todd was extremely angry but didn't want to hear, or listen to, any of the details. So Summer continued listening to Tina, and encouraged her to make an appointment with the Equal Employment Opportunity Commission (EEOC). Summer also called a lawyer for Tina. Tina was confused and uncertain about what to do. She didn't want to leave the job she loved, and she was living in Frank's daughter's townhouse. Tina was in the EEOC's office for over four hours before she began to fully understand, and accept that what Frank was doing was wrong, and she finally agreed to file a formal complaint. After the EEOC meeting, she met with the lawyer, who agreed to take her case on contingency.

The lawyer instructed Tina to write every little detail she could remember regarding Frank's inappropriate behavior toward her. Tina realized she could not emotionally wait for, or testify at, an open jury trial, especially since she was still living in Frank's daughter's townhouse. So she settled out of court for an "undisclosed sum of money." The money meant nothing to Tina. She had to leave the job she loved and lost a family she thought cared about her. And she had to uproot everything and move. Tina would never have left LVM had it not been for the owner's despicable acts. As part of the settlement, Tina asked for mandatory sexual harassment training for all LVM employees, and counseling for Frank and his family. Unfortunately, all she got was hush money.

Although Tina had not yet come to recognize the fullness of her value as God's creation, she finally understood no boss or authority figure had the right to do what Frank did to her. Tina still had a great need for love and acceptance, and began to wonder if there was more. What could ever fill the void?

It's OK to say no. We need not allow others to take advantage of us, or treat us in an unworthy manner.

Keep your heart with all diligence,
*For out of it **spring** the issues of life.*
(Proverbs 4:23)

***Let** your speech always **be** with grace,*
seasoned with salt, that you may know
how you ought to answer each one.
(Colossians 4:6)

Are there unnecessary TAN threads
being woven in your life right now?
How does God want you to respond? [178]

_____
_____
_____
_____
_____
_____
_____
_____
_____
_____
_____
_____
_____
_____
_____
_____
_____
_____
_____
_____

Have you learned to forgive those who have sinned against you? Don't allow unforgiveness to steal the inner peace Jesus died to provide. God will take care of those who have offended us; all we can do is pray for them.

Then He said to the disciples,
*"It is impossible that no offenses should come, but woe to **him** through whom they do come! It would be better for him if a millstone were hung around his neck, and he were thrown into the sea, than that he should offend one of these little ones. Take heed to yourselves. If your brother sins against you, rebuke him; and if he repents, forgive him. And if he sins against you seven times in a day, and seven times in a day returns to you, saying, 'I repent,' you shall forgive him."*
(Luke 17:1-4)

Are you holding any unforgiveness in your heart for those who brought the TAN threads? [179]

_____

_____

_____

_____

_____

_____

_____

_____

_____

_____

_____

_____

_____

_____

We are of great value to God. More valuable than any of His other creatures and creations.

"Are not five sparrows sold for two copper coins?
And not one of them is forgotten before God.
But the very hairs of your head are all numbered.
Do not fear therefore; you are of more value
than many sparrows. (Luke 12:6-7)

What is TAN about your life right now? [180]

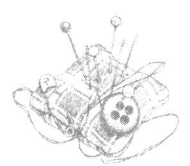

PERIWINKLE BLUE
Creative Expression

Tina painted quite often when she was living in the townhouse in Torrance. She even set up one of the bedrooms and half of the two-car garage as art studios, spaces where she could paint uninhibited. Tina obtained her first business license and, though she was working full time at LVM, started a side business she called The Art Studios of Tina Ann (ASTA). Tina submitted her art to various galleries, and some of her paintings and photographs were exhibited in various U.S. art galleries. Painting helped Tina release a lot of emotional pain, anger, and suffering, pouring herself out upon the canvas. Painting wasn't just a creative outlet for her, it was an emotional outlet. Tina would crank up the stereo, crack open a beer or two, and dance and paint to her heart's content. Tina often thought about different ways to put more of her soul, of herself, into her paintings, and came up with an idea to do exactly that. Tina's signature paintings were actual body prints. Picking the perfect size canvas, she would pull out tubes of acrylic paint, choosing whatever colors inspired her at the time. She would drench the canvas with water, dip the brush in paint, and swoop away at the canvas. She enjoyed watching the color spread as it hit the wet canvas, forming the background of the painting. After the first coat dried, Tina would make various kinds of body prints in a darker tone. For once in her life Tina was pleased with the results of her creations. She had succeeded in putting her heart, soul and body into these paintings. Tina was happy to hear the delightful comments about her artwork, especially considering the fact that no actual body parts could be distinguished.

Tina began attending fine art trade shows, and met a man who offered to be her manager. Although her media of choice had always been acrylic paint, Tina's manager encouraged her to experiment with different media. Tina used everything from car wax, resin, and house paint, to stain, bondo, and anything else she could find laying around in her garage. She found this new work freeing, and obtained some very interesting results.

Tina turned her deep inner turmoil from the sexual molestation into works of art. Dark reds and blacks expressed the pain and emptiness she felt. The grand size—the smallest was six feet by four feet—expressed the overwhelming help-lessness Tina encountered before she began standing up for herself. Although dark and dreadful, this series of paintings was prominently exhibited from the front window of a huge building smack dab in the middle of Sunset Blvd. in Los Angeles. Tina was proud of her creative accomplishment.

In exploring some of the difficult times of loss, Tina created a series of paintings which included a kind of memorial to Tina's family, friends, and loved ones who had died. For each person memorialized, Tina painted a background that would coincide with a specific memory—a sailboat for her grandparents, a sunflower for her friend Candy, red roses for Shawn—and poetic words of expression about Tina's loved one added in black paint. These paintings were exhibited in Northern California at a show called "Stop the Violence."

Tina actively painted and exhibited in the early to mid nineties—from a series of paintings of flowers and light subject matter exhibited at a coffee house in Orange, California, to the emotionally dark paintings exhibited in Los Angeles. Tina's paintings have also been exhibited in Washington, DC and Chicago, Illinois, and her photographs at a gallery in Long Beach, California. Tina still didn't believe she was a very good artist and was rarely satisfied with the works she created.

Tina's more recent works have an entirely different feel to them. There's no more a darkness or sense of despair, but rather lightness and joy. Because of the change the Lord has made in her heart and life, Tina got rid of all the dark paintings, and now attempts to reveal the light and love of Christ in nearly everything she creates. One of the first paintings Tina made after receiving Christ into her life was a small, wilted, black rose, closed and frozen, with icicles hanging from dead petals in the lower left corner of the small canvas. Above the dead and frozen rose Tina painted a large, white rose with pink accents, in full bloom with drops of morning dew on the petals, and bright green leaves; bright, alive, and warm. When asked about it, Tina says, "It's sort of a depiction of what Jesus has done in my life. He pulled me out of a dark, dead, and frozen life, and brought me into His marvelous light. He made me alive in Him, and filled me with the warmth of the ever-burning Holy Spirit, melting the icicles that had formed upon my heart."

> *For we are His workmanship,*
> *created in Christ Jesus for good works,*
> *which God prepared beforehand*
> *that we should walk in them.*
> *(Ephesians 2:10)*

Tina loves to sing, and can't remember a time when she didn't sing, whether childhood songs, singing along to Shawn's rock 'n' roll records when they were growing up, with the car radio, or popular songs in high school. Being surrounded by music growing up inspired Tina's love for singing. She started playing the flute in grammar school, but quit when she started high school. Tina didn't want to be a band geek.

Martha played violin in the Palos Verdes Peninsula Symphony, and when they were children, Tina and her siblings were dragged to their mom's concerts. Tina didn't appreciate classical music then the way she does now, and usually fell asleep during Martha's concerts. Tina did, however, look forward to the hot fudge sundaes they got at the Wooden Shoe restaurant after the concerts. Larry's jazz band rehearsed at the house every Wednesday night, but Tina didn't appreciate their music, either. She really didn't enjoy any genres other than folk-rock and pure rock 'n' roll. But she got to stay up late when Larry's band rehearsed, which was great. Tina's brother, Todd, is a singer songwriter, and Tina was privileged to sing backup for one of his bands when she was in her early twenties.

When Tina started going to Rolling Hills Covenant Church[1], she joined the choir and, though not required, she wanted to learn how to read music again. Tina had completely forgotten how since she quit playing the flute. Larry was writing a musical at the time. Tina helped her stepdad with the typing and graphics for his musical, so she asked if he would mind teaching her how to read music again so she could sing some of the songs he had written for the female characters. Not only did he agree, he even wrote some of the songs specifically in her key. Tina had never before experienced such a wonderful time of father-daughter bonding.

Most of the time when Tina worked on songs with her dad, Martha was nice enough to stay in another room so she wouldn't be tempted to interfere. Unfortunately, that didn't last long and there came a point when Martha expressed her desire to sing a song or two. Tina so treasured the time and attention she was getting from her stepdad, time and attention she had so longed for as a child, but she also realized her mom might need the attention even more than Tina did.

Before long, Rick's wife expressed her desire to sing some of the songs. Then it was Todd's wife and sons. When the time came to record some of the songs, Todd was doing all the recording, being a musician and techie. Tina had taken some private voice lessons before recording, and got one of the songs down and recorded fine, but the time came for Tina to sing another song to record. Todd has a tendency to get easily frustrated and this was no exception. The recording was taking longer than expected because Tina wasn't hitting all the notes exactly, which Todd definitely let her know. They stopped recording, and a few weeks later Todd recorded his wife, Summer, singing the very same song; the song Tina's stepdad had written for her to sing.

Tina was deeply hurt and saddened and the bonding time she had been experiencing with her stepfather was gone. No more one-on-one time with her dad.

Tina realizes her family had no idea how much the singing project with her stepdad meant to her, and is sure they had no intention of hurting her. Nevertheless, afterward Tina was afraid to sing, even in church. Tina listened to the lie that she was tone deaf, and had a terrible voice. Thankfully, some years later, using a sister in Christ to test Tina's vocal ability, the Lord healed Tina's wound. Tina *can* sing, even on key, and was blessed again to sing in a worship band for a ministry that God used to heal many of Tina's past hurts.

> *Oh, sing to the LORD a new song! Sing to the LORD, all the earth. Sing to the LORD, bless His name; Proclaim the good news of His salvation from day to day. Declare His glory among the nations, His wonders among all peoples. (Psalm 96:1-3)*

In 2008, Tina started knitting scarves as Christmas gifts. Tina treated the vast array of yarns available like paint upon a canvas and knitting became another art form for her. One evening, Tina was out window shopping in Hollywood Riviera (Redondo Beach) wearing one of her scarves. A small boutique owner admired the scarf Tina was wearing. Tina told the boutique owner that she had made the scarf herself and the owner asked Tina if she would knit some for her to sell in her boutique. Tina began thinking of ways to market her creations. She created a logo and a brand, TERI, which is an acronym for Touch Embrace Renew Inspire. Over the next few weeks Tina knitted scarves for the shop, tying handmade labels with the TERI logo to each scarf. Tina also designed and printed brochures and posters, and even put up a myTERI website. The boutique shop owner bought every single scarf Tina had knitted and even wanted more. Tina created window posters to display at the boutique and then knit, knit, knitted away. When Tina returned with the second batch of scarves, the owner again bought every last one, and even requested more for another location in Hermosa Beach. Remember, Tina's no seamstress; she had only recently taught herself how to knit. The appeal of her scarves didn't come from fancy knots or weaving, it came from Tina's keen sense of color, the unique yarns she selected, and the signed and numbered tags Tina had hand tied to each scarf. So important had the signed tag become, shop owners would look for the tag before noticing the designs or colors used; no tag, no purchase.

Tina's scarves had become another type of artwork. She knitted and creatively packaged over eighty scarves to hand out to actors, producers, directors, and other film industry professionals for the Temecula Valley International Film Festival, and they were a big hit. When the opportunity arose for Tina to exhibit some of her scarves at one of the biggest garment industry trade shows, she decided against it since she didn't have the capability to fill large orders for large department stores. Tina still knits a scarf or two every now and then but stopped marketing myTERI scarves after realizing she could not meet the demand if she continued getting more orders.

As Tina reflects back on all the projects she started but didn't finish, the businesses she let go of, and the numerous opportunities others work so hard to find, she's recognized how blessed she's been, but never appreciated. Tina had many wonderful opportunities to earn a living being creative but, not being a risk taker and never believing in herself enough, Tina self-sabotaged every opportunity the Lord presented to her.

Will Tina ever have enough faith to step out and trust God, who so graciously bestowed upon her a creatively passionate business mind? Well, she is determined to share the story God has woven into her life.

*Trust in the LORD with all your heart, And lean
not on your own understanding; In __all__ your ways
acknowledge Him, And He shall direct your paths.
(Proverbs 3:5-6, emphasis mine)*

Are you trusting God with the PERIWINKLE BLUE threads of your tapestry? [181]

_____
_____
_____
_____
_____
_____
_____
_____
_____
_____
_____
_____
_____
_____
_____
_____
_____
_____
_____
_____
_____
_____
_____
_____
_____
_____

For we are His workmanship, created in Christ Jesus
for good works, which God prepared beforehand
that we should walk in them. (Ephesians 2:10)

What are some of the PERIWINKLE BLUE threads God has gifted you with? Are you using them for His glory? [182]

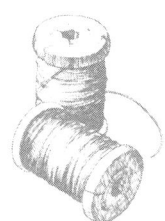

IVORY

From Twisted Truth to Divine Revelation

While Tina was in limbo with her job at Lens Vision due to the sexual harassment, she went to a lot of concerts with her friend, Trent, the videographer she hired for LVM. Trent did a lot of video work for famous heavy metal rock bands such as Megadeth, Dokken, and Lynch Mob. Although Tina didn't really care much for heavy metal music, she had a lot of fun partying with Trent and his rock star friends. Some of them did pretty weird stuff spiritually but, what the heck, they were rock stars so it must be cool, right?

One weekend Tina went to a BBQ with Trent at the home of his friends, Moon and Jade. Tina found them a bit odd, but Moon was a drummer and, since they seemed nice enough, she shrugged it off to typical weirdness so often seen in people living around Hollywood. The fact that Moon and Jade lived in a secluded area was strange enough to Tina, but their serious belief in aliens and burning of sage to ward off evil spirits made them much more odd. Other musicians showed up for the BBQ and they all jammed in a ragged old barn on the property. Being a music lover, Tina enjoyed sitting in the old barn listening to them, but the snake that was nailed to the wall gave her the heebie jeebies. Earlier, Moon had caught a snake in the yard. He killed it, chopped off its head, and nailed both the head and the body to the wall of the barn. While they were jamming, Moon pointed to the snake's body and proclaimed, "Look, it's still moving." To her relief, Tina never saw it move.

Tina doesn't recall what possessed her to go to a psychic bookstore, but not long after spending time with Trent and his friends at the BBQ, she went to The Psychic Eye bookshop (since renamed the New Age Bookshop, a good indicator of the true root of the New Age movement). Tina felt a little afraid, and very self-conscious, when she first walked in, but knowing the people she had been hanging out with probably frequented such stores, she reasoned her fear away. After being in the store for a little while and seeing how many people were shopping, Tina's fear subsided and she felt comfortable. Yikes! She wasn't really sure why she was there or what she was looking for, but after about an hour looking around, Tina purchased two candles, one for love and one for money. Each candle came with an instruction sheet, but Tina still called one of the men she had met at the BBQ to ask exactly how to use the candles. He instructed Tina to light the candle, hold it in front of her, concentrate on what she desired, and repeatedly read out loud the incantation from the instruction sheet. Tina did as he instructed, not realizing this is one of the things the Bible calls witchcraft! (See *Leviticus 20:6.*)

Tina had the dream of all dreams that night. She dreamt she was lying on a bed in her parents' bedroom in the house where she grew up. She was speaking some evil language, as though she was possessed like Linda Blair in the original *Exorcist* movie while creepy, wicked looking people were leaning over her waving their hands and chanting incantations. The dream shifted, and suddenly Tina was in the bedroom she shared with her two sisters growing up. The room was filled with a brilliant white light shining through a thin, fog-like mist. The light was so bright, so luminous, it is humanly indescribable; a radiant, white light unimaginable. A man in a white robe sat on the floor of the room, praying for Tina. Although she couldn't make out who the figure was through the fog, because of the results of her dream, Tina likes to imagine that perhaps it was Jesus.

When Tina woke up, she had uncanny spiritual discernment. Looking around her apartment, she realized it was full of occult influences. Tina realized the act of meditating and chanting with the candles she had purchased at the occult book shop was witchcraft. Tina also recognized that many of the books she owned were influenced by the occult—coffee table books about witches, warlocks, fairies, and the like. Tina hadn't been to church in over ten years, hadn't prayed in over five and, since she wasn't truly a born-again believer, never cracked open a Bible. No one had ever taught her the difference between what the Bible teaches is bad or evil, and what is good or holy, but Tina was well aware, and even had uncanny insight to discern between the various religious cults and Christianity based on the truth of salvation through Christ alone. Most of the people Tina had been hanging out with were following ideas opposite of what the Bible teaches as being good, and this initially made Tina fearful. So many of her friends were living in deception, especially considering it was the very onset of the New Age movement. I realize this all sounds a bit strange, but God knew exactly what it would take to get through Tina's ultra imaginative mind, and so He did, loud and clear. He knew how much the movie *The Exorcist* frightened Tina when she saw it in her teens. The dream may have scared Tina, but at the same time it opened her eyes to the Truth.

Later that day, Tina had a meeting with the counselor she was meeting with regarding the sexual harassment case. She decided she would tell the counselor about her dream. Tina had no idea the counselor was a Christian. When she told her about the dream, the counselor responded with, "It sounds like you're under a spiritual attack. You should go buy yourself a Bible." That's all it took. Afterward, Tina went straight to the nearest Christian bookstore and bought a Bible. While there she shared with a few of the store's employees and prayed with them; renouncing the witchcraft, repenting of her sin, asking for forgiveness, and turning her life over to Jesus Christ. Tina had never really understood much of what was written in the Bible, even with all the times she had gone to church throughout her life, but following her dream and the many prayers afterward, Tina had an extraordinary understanding of every single jot and tittle she read in God's word. For the first time in her life Tina fully understood how much God loved her. She couldn't get enough of God's word, and read the Bible for hours every day. Tina cried tears of joy, often with outstretched arms, while listening and singing to worship music, thanking the Lord for the love He so graciously bestowed upon her. Tina couldn't believe Jesus would suffer and die for a wretch like her, but He did!

At the same time after the dream, Tina's desire for alcohol, partying and sex was completely removed. She had been drinking every day for at least a year, and had no qualms about having sex with nearly any man she dated, as she equated sex with love, so Tina knew this was a miracle. She started going to church on a regular basis, eventually finding her way to Rolling Hills Covenant Church (RHCC) in Rolling Hills Estates. Tina went forward and prayed the sinner's prayer again during a dramatic play and outreach called *The Choice*, on October 8th, 1994. She was baptized at RHCC on February 19th, 1995, by Pastor Vergil Best.

Tina couldn't hold this wonderful news in; she had to share the truth of Christ with everyone she knew, and even those she didn't. Tina didn't want anyone to die without knowing what God did for them in and through Jesus. Tina didn't want those she knows and loves spending eternity in hell. Tina made sack lunches, complete with a New Testament, and went out on the streets of Los Angeles where she handed out the lunches, shared the love of Christ, and prayed for the homeless she encountered. Tina was blessed to witness one of the women she had given a sack to reading the little Bible as Tina drove around the corner before heading home. Sadly, the day ended with a woman refusing to accept the sack lunch and, in response to Tina telling her Jesus loves her, wrathfully claimed to be Jesus herself. Thank God for His protection from the enemy's schemes to discourage Tina, through the prayers and encouragement of her brothers and sisters in Christ. The Lord also blessed Tina with the time, money, and inspiration to organize and fund an outreach concert at a nearby public housing facility. A Christian band called *The Gospel Gangstaz* performed, and the gospel message was preached pointing the residents to the truth of Jesus. Tina served meals at homeless shelters, prayed for people, taught Sunday school, and did anything she could for the Lord, out of gratitude and love for Him. Tina was also blessed with the Lord initially placing her in a church that not only teaches and preaches the word, but is creative. Tina got cast in a large production, similar to *The Pageant of the Masters*[11] in Laguna Beach, called *The Pageant of Our Lord*[12] where human beings are made up to portray pieces of artwork. What a blessing that the Lord allows us to serve Him in ways we so enjoy!

Following her salvation experience, Tina continued meeting with the counselor, but they only discussed the legalities and details left to complete regarding her sexual harassment at LVM. She only had a few more meetings with her lawyer prior to the final settlement. Realizing the importance of prayer, before the mediation, Tina called one of her friends from church and they prayed together for a God-led outcome. For the mediation Tina met with her lawyer, a mediator, Frank's lawyer, and Frank himself, face-to-face in a neutral location in Los Angeles. The lawyer's goal was to settle out of court. In retrospect, Tina sometimes wishes she would have taken a stronger stand, as the settlement did little but slap Frank on the hand, as if to say "bad boy." The only requests of Tina's finally agreed upon were being able to write good-bye letters to Frank's family members, permission to break the lease with Frank's daughter, and some money. None of those things did a darn thing to heal Tina's hurt, or teach Frank what he had done was wrong and unacceptable. But she was so full of joy with her new love—Jesus—that she didn't realize just how much she had lost. Tina had enjoyed her job at LVM more than any other.

One stipulation of the settlement barred Frank from contacting Tina in any way, shape, or form. Months later Tina was out shopping with her mother when she noticed Frank walking in. Tina's mom suggested she talk to him, even suggesting Tina might go back to work for him. Tina actually considered it for a moment and, because she was still subconsciously attempting to please her family, she did approach him and said, "Hi." They spoke for a moment, and Frank acted sympathetic. Tina realized she was right back to her patterns when she allowed him to touch her in unacceptable ways. She immediately became a submissive little girl, wanting her daddy's love. Tina fully understood what had transpired, and would dare not approach him again; she wasn't strong enough. Frank passed away in 2002.

After moving out of Frank's daughter's townhouse, Tina stayed with her parents while she looked to purchase a house in Orange County. At the same time, the trial for the man who murdered Linda's husband was beginning. To support Linda, Tina went to court with her on the first day. Tina had planned to continue house shopping the next day, but changed her plans after the Lord helped her realize the most important thing for her to do was to support her friend. So, Tina put her house shopping on hold, and attended the trial with Linda. The perpetrator was found guilty of first degree murder, attempted murder, assault with a deadly weapon, breaking and entering, rape, sexual assault, and burglary.

The penalty phase of the trial came up next, and the video Trent made showing what Linda's life was like before the horrific event in comparison to her life after the crime, was allowed, setting a precedent as the first time such a video was accepted. Victim's statement videos are now used in other penalty phases. At the conclusion of the penalty phase of the trial, after considering all the evidence and the severity of the crime, the jury voted unanimously in favor of the death penalty.

The death penalty sentence gave Linda some relief, although she still misses her husband and the life she had with him before this horrific tragedy. Linda has raised her daughter wonderfully. Brittney is one of the top students in her college, and both she and her mother are embarking on new chapters of their lives. Tina can't imagine how difficult forgiveness must be for Linda. God calls us to forgive, even our enemies. But to forgive the terrible man whose actions ripped Linda's life to shreds; is that possible? Only through the miraculous power of the Holy Spirit is forgiveness in any situation be possible. As Jesus looked down upon those who nailed Him to the cross, in pain and agony, He said, *"Father, forgive them, for they know not what they do."*[13] Thanks to Jesus, we too, through the power of the Holy Spirit can forgive those who have hurt us.

Though Tina had lived a life full of sin and darkness, in His love and grace the Lord chose to point her toward the Truth. Just in the nick of time, as Tina had begun to journey down a road full of lies and darkness in the form of different types of spiritualism which has deceived many, especially the youth.

He has delivered us from the power of darkness and conveyed us into the kingdom of the Son of His love, in whom we have redemption through His blood, the forgiveness of sins. (Colossians 1:13-14)

Have you experienced the IVORY shade of God's great deliverance? [183]

Lighting special candles and meditating on them with words for power, money, love, revenge, and other desires, is witchcraft, plain and simple; a lie from the enemy, which is rooted in the occult. Don't let media influences that glorify witchcraft, vampires, black magic and the like deceive you into thinking such practices are harmless.

*Beloved, do not believe every spirit, but test the spirits, whether they are of God; because many false prophets have gone out into the world. By this you know the Spirit of God: Every spirit that confesses that Jesus Christ has come in the flesh is of God, and every spirit that does not confess that Jesus Christ has come in the flesh is not of God. And this is the **spirit** of the Antichrist, which you have heard was coming, and is now already in the world.   (1 John 4:1-3)*

Have you been deceived by the lies of this world? Do you need some IVORY threads of God's deliverance, mercy, and grace? [184]

God so loved Tina He sent His only begotten Son to die so she might live. Tina is absolutely amazed at the extent of the love, mercy, and grace God has for us; she had only one way to respond—repent (turn away from) her sin, put her faith and trust in Jesus, and start living her life for Him who so loved her. And she needed to shout it from the rooftops!

*For God so loved the **world***
(that includes me; that includes you!)
that He gave His only begotten Son, that whoever believes in Him should not perish but have everlasting life. For God did not send His Son into the world to condemn the world, but that the world through Him might be saved.
(John 3:16-17, emphasis mine)

List some of the ways God has revealed some IVORY hues of love in your life. [185]

_____
_____
_____
_____
_____
_____
_____
_____
_____
_____
_____
_____
_____

See also *John 14:6; Romans 5:8;* and *Ephesians 2:1-9.*

Rejoice the soul of Your servant,
For to You, O Lord, I lift up my soul.
*For You, Lord, **are** good, and ready to forgive,*
And abundant in mercy to all those who call upon You.
(Psalm 86:4-5)

Are there more IVORY threads that God is weaving into your tapestry? [186]

ORANGE
The Excitement of the Journey

Tina had every intention of buying a house in Orange County when Linda's trial was over, but God had another plan. Tina had become more and more involved at RHCC, and when the opportunity to go on a tour through Israel, Greece, Turkey, and Rome, led by senior pastor Byron MacDonald arose, she jumped at the chance! Tina was blessed to have the time and finances, only three months after surrendering her life to Jesus, to go to Israel and see, first hand, exactly where Jesus walked. One of Tina's best memories from the trip was taking communion at the Garden Tomb. The Garden Tomb was discovered in 1883 by British General Charles Gordon,[14] who thought it to be the actual tomb where Jesus was buried and resurrected. *"Now in the place where He was crucified there was a garden, and in the garden a new tomb in which no one had yet been laid" (John 19:41).* Celebrating the Lord's Supper in one of the places Jesus is thought to have been buried and resurrected was an emotional experience. Not one person in the group (even the men) had a dry eye. The area surrounding the Garden Tomb is beautiful, truly a garden setting, with no other tombs in the area. The hill on which the Garden Tomb is situated resembles a human skull. As it states in *John 19:17-18, "And He, bearing His cross, went out to a place called the Place of a Skull, which is called in Hebrew, Golgotha, where they crucified Him, and two others with Him, one on either side, and Jesus in the center."*

Another especially memorable area was the Garden of Gethsemane. Tina has an affinity for trees, they're the subject matter of many of her photos and drawings, and the ancient olive trees at Gethsemane are breathtaking. The old, gnarled olive trees fascinated Tina. The older an olive tree is, the broader and more gnarled is its trunk. Olive trees don't have rings, so their age cannot be precisely determined through ring count but, through carbon dating, scholars estimate the age of the olive trees in the Garden of Gethsemane to be between one and two thousand years old. The Garden of Gethsemane is where Jesus prayed the night of his betrayal and arrest.[15] According to the record in Luke, Christ's despair in Gethsemane was so deep, He sweated drops of blood.[16] Imagining Jesus off by Himself praying, the night He knew He would be betrayed, increased Tina's understanding of the love Jesus has for humanity.

Though Tina had already been baptized, she felt led to give her testimony and be baptized again in the Jordan River; talk about a once in a lifetime experience! So was taking a boat across the Sea of Galilee, letting down the sail and, in the middle of this peaceful body of water, listening to Pastor Byron read from Matthew and preach the Word of God. The Sea of Galilee is where Jesus conducted much of His ministry and where He called four of his early disciples, the fishermen Peter, Andrew, John, and James.[17] Tina stood on the same hill where Jesus gave His Sermon on the Mount.[18] Tina's group also visited Bethlehem, the birthplace of Jesus,[19] Corinth in Greece,[20] Ephesus in Turkey,[21] Patmos, the small Greek island in the Aegean Sea where John was in prison when he received the Revelation of Jesus,[22] Rome, and many other places where Jesus actually walked.

The Lord tugged at Tina's heartstrings regarding missions while she was in Israel. Tina was taking a picture of an old Muslim woman, who was small in stature but large in character, standing outside the Dome of the Rock. The old woman couldn't speak a word of English, but smiled at Tina, allowing her to take the picture. The woman then reached down and removed a small, golden brooch from the dress she wore. Reaching out to Tina, the woman attempted to give her the golden camel brooch. As kind a gesture as it was, Tina couldn't accept such a generous gift from a total stranger. Tina felt such love for the woman, and wanted to share with her about Jesus, but Tina didn't speak Arabic.

Instead, she gave the woman a hug and a smile, and headed on her way with the rest of the group. Later, when Tina shared her experience with Pastor Byron's wife, Lynda, and her deep desire to tell the woman about Jesus, Lynda explained it was against the law to share your Christian faith openly in many parts of the Middle East, especially among Muslims. Tina's heart was broken! All the traveling Tina had done over the years made so much sense. In all her travels Tina had never been interested in going on tours and hanging out with the tourists. She wanted to learn about the nationals and their reality. She wanted to learn about the culture and the country.

When Tina returned home, she met with the missions pastor at RHCC, who pointed her in the direction of missions and evangelism among Muslims. Tina enrolled in a program through RHCC called Scripture and Leadership Training (SALT), and took various mission related and biblically based courses. When Tina applied to serve with a well known mission agency, she was accepted. As part of the preparation for serving in the Middle East, an environment hostile to Christians, Tina was required to take numerous cognitive and psychological tests. The results revealed Tina to be a bit on the submissive side which would be an issue serving in a potentially hostile environment. Tina did work on assertiveness, but realized later she hadn't allowed God's word to go deep enough to give her the strength and tools necessary for setting vital boundaries.

Tina visited three countries in the Middle East and prayed intensely before deciding in which country, and with which team, she would serve. She spent the summer in a full cultural immersion program for missionaries in training, during which Tina lived with a Christian Egyptian couple in Pasadena. Prospective missionaries serving various people groups met and studied daily, and were assigned to learn all they could about the culture in which they were to serve. This is referred to as contextualization. Tina attended an Egyptian, Arabic speaking Christian church in Pasadena to learn Arabic and about the Arab culture. Tina also visited various mosques to gain empathy and understanding about Islam, so she could be a better witness to them.

Tina was the only person in the cultural immersion program preparing to go to the Middle East, and was assigned to find and conduct field studies of the Armenian neighborhood in Pasadena. Tina was provided no information or location details regarding where her assigned neighborhood was exactly. Pasadena is a fairly large city and Tina was somewhat intimidated at the prospect. All the fear and trepidation subsided when, after inquiring at a Pasadena gas station, she entered a neighborhood where all the signs were written in Arabic. Tina felt like she was back in the Middle East! Her first day out, she found her assigned neighborhood and Tina spent two hours interviewing a woman in a neighborhood jewelry store. The woman invited Tina to stay and have coffee with her, meeting the woman's daughter when she arrived at the store after school. Building relationships came very easily for Tina. In attending morning meetings with the missionaries studying other cultures, she learned many of the others had difficulty finding their assigned neighborhoods and building relationships. Tina later realized the Lord had given her a wonderful gift to approach and meet people fairly easily.

The missionary students were instructed to find a mentor who could teach them about the culture and language they were studying. In this area Tina had difficulty. Tina ended up asking an Egyptian man she had met at the Arab Egyptian Christian church she attended. His American name was Tomas. His Arab Egyptian name was Tihrak. Tomas had converted to Christianity from Islam, fled Egypt to Cyprus, and eventually came to the United States to go to school. He taught Tina a lot about Islam, sharing his testimony about a dream he had which brought him to the truth of Jesus, similar to how God got hold of Tina. He shared with her his desire to return to the Middle East to serve as a missionary. Tina and Tomas started dating and, because she was learning the culture and wanted to act accordingly and do everything as they would in the Arab world, the two became engaged. According to the pastor of the Egyptian church, a man and woman in the area of the Middle East she would be serving would not be allowed to go out on a date unchaperoned unless they were formally engaged. Tomas gave Tina a ring and they announced their engagement to the church. In Tina's mind, their engagement was really just a "permission slip" to date, but in Tomas's mind they were on their way to the altar of marriage even though they had only known each other a little over a month.

Because of the mission training's focus on total immersion, students were instructed not to communicate with friends or family members, in an attempt to stick to the language and culture they were learning. Tina was fine with this restriction, as it also taught her discretion regarding where she would be serving. Because she was planning to serve in an area where Christian missionaries are not allowed, for the safety of all Christians who serve there Tina was instructed not to disclose where she would be serving to her own church, or even the missions pastor.

While Tina was in the training program, two Egyptian friends of hers from RHCC, Nagy and Safy, had taken a team on a short-term mission trip to Egypt. Nagy was a wonderful man on fire for the Lord, and was so excited about Tina's desire to serve in the Middle East. He had been tutoring Tina in Arabic before she left for the missionary training program. He and his wife were very kind to Tina, and Nagy was proud of her for trying to learn his language. During the mission trip to their homeland, Nagy had a heart attack at dinner one night and died suddenly. He died in the land in which he was born, doing what he loved to do—sharing Christ. The Egyptian couple Tina was staying with at the time knew Nagy and Safy, as did many others in the Egyptian church she was attending. The leaders of the missionary immersion program and Tina's team leaders in the Middle East allowed her to attend Nagy's memorial service. Tina was absolutely devastated. But, although she was sad and knew she would miss Nagy, there was a new joy in the midst of the loss, because Tina knew without a doubt Nagy was home in heaven, in the presence of Jesus.

After completing the missions training program, Tina and Tomas decided to get to know each other more in her environment, so Tomas started attending church services at RHCC with Tina. Since he lived a distance away and didn't drive, Tina allowed him to sleep on her couch on occasion—her first mistake. Tomas started showing his true colors one night when he absolutely insisted on going upstairs to sleep with Tina in her bed because there were ants downstairs. She actually let him—mistake number two—and he tried to have sex with her. Tina stopped him before he went too far, but it was still sin! She should have never let him stay at her house in the first place. The couple confessed their sin to the missions pastor, and Tina found a male friend from the church who agreed to allow Tomas to stay with him. Tomas became very angry as a result, so Tina broke off the engagement. Tina obviously hadn't totally worked through her submissiveness, and this was another example of her inability to set boundaries. The Lord was teaching her another tough lesson. Following the breakup, Tina gained fifty pounds, and weighed more than she ever had. Tina used her weight to protect herself from men and the possibility of getting hurt again.

Not long after their breakup, the door for Tina to serve overseas was closed, as the necessary financial support did not come in as expected. Then, the attack on the Twin Towers and the Pentagon happened (9/11/2001). The Lord protected Tina from making the huge mistake of marrying an overly aggressive man. Oh, how He loves us! And, the doors to serve in the Middle East were closed possibly as a result of her sin, but also as God's protection from a mission Tina was not ready for. Praise God for disciplining those He loves just like a loving parent disciplines their children.

> *"My son, do not despise the chastening of the LORD,*
> *Nor be discouraged when you are rebuked by Him;*
> *For whom the LORD loves He chastens, And scourges*
> *every son whom He receives." (Hebrews 12:5-6)*

September 11, 2001 . . . Tina was working on a Christian graphics project in her home office when her mom called and asked if she had seen the news proclaiming, "They're attacking us." When Tina turned on the news she couldn't believe what she was seeing; the tail end of a commercial jet liner sticking out the side of one of the Twin Towers in New York. Thousands of innocent people died that day. Tina's heart broke for the families who had lost loved ones. She was also saddened by the thought of how the incident might negatively affect relationships built between Christian missionaries and those they had gone to share the love of Christ with.

Tina wasn't surprised to hear an Islamic fundamentalist group was taking responsibility. She had learned a lot about Islamic fundamentalism in preparation to serve among Muslims. The terrible tragedy brought Tina to her knees to pray for those who lost loved ones and for those in the Middle East who had yet to truly hear and receive the Truth of Christ. Americans have learned a lot more about Islam and the Middle East since the 9/11 attacks. Before that infamous event, Tina had shared with friends and family how blessed we are in America to have the religious freedom to worship in public, carry a Bible, talk openly about Jesus, attend church, and so much more. Tina's family didn't understand or believe her when she had shared with them that people are actually killed for simply professing Christ in some countries. As an American, born and raised, it's difficult to comprehend the fact that many Christians have been forced to flee their homelands for fear of their lives. Prior to 9/11 it was hard for many Americans to believe that it's actually illegal to be Christian in some countries, a crime punishable by death.

During her trip to the Arab Gulf, Tina visited a women's prison where she met two women imprisoned for things they would never have been punished for in America. One woman, a Pakistani, was imprisoned for adultery, after being turned in by a man who had repeatedly raped her. Many Pakistanis came to this particular country to serve as maids and nannies. Upon arrival, this woman was picked up by her chaperon, who proceeded to take her to a small apartment where he held her captive, raped her, and then invited his friends over to do the same. When he got tired of her, he turned her in for adultery. At the testimony of one man, she was imprisoned, received 100 lashings, and had no idea when she would be released. The woman who took Tina to visit the women in prison was part of a Christian ministry, and had shared the gospel with this Pakistani woman, who then gave her life to Christ prior to the lashings. This lovely, innocent prisoner attributed feeling no pain during her punishment to the Lord. Her horrific wounds took mere days to heal, a great witness to the other expatriate Pakistani women in the prison, as they had seen other women's wounds take three weeks or longer to heal. Many gave their lives to Christ as a result.

Another woman prisoner Tina met was a national to the Middle East country she was visiting. Tina couldn't speak openly with her as a woman guard, wearing the hijab, burqa, and abaya—clothed and completely covered, face and all, in black—wouldn't leave her side. Although free, this particular country still practiced Islamic sharia law, the code of conduct or religious law of Islam—precepts set forth in the Quran—and nationals were strictly watched, as it was mandatory for them to abide by sharia law. Tina had spoken to this girl's mother while she was waiting for them to bring the prisoners out for visiting time, and got her daughter's story then. Her daughter had been attending college in England and came home to visit her family when her father was hospitalized due to serious heart complications. At a hotel bar where alcohol was served, the young woman sat with a sheikh's son who was drinking alcohol, though she herself was not. She was imprisoned for being unchaperoned in a bar with a man, and the man she was sitting with was imprisoned for drinking alcohol. Her mother was greatly saddened her daughter was in prison. She was fearful her daughter would be lashed, and had no idea when she would be released. She was also concerned about her husband, still very ill and in the hospital. Unfortunately, Tina could not share the gospel with either the mother or daughter with the prison guard so closely watching.

> *Blessed **are** those who are persecuted for righteousness' sake, For theirs is the kingdom of heaven. (Matthew 5:10)*

Early in her Christian walk, the Lord graciously allowed Tina to work with and for other Christians. She feels as though God had her in a protective bubble, shielding her from the influences of the outside world. Tina worked part-time as the program director for Love INC (Love In the Name of Christ), a World Vision ministry.[23] Their mission is mobilization of the Church to transform lives and communities In the Name of Christ. Tina also did some freelance graphic design and was blessed to work with Rose Publishing,[24] RHCC, and numerous Christian ministries. The graphic work was a rewarding and wonderful creative outlet for Tina but it didn't bring in quite enough money to pay the bills. The funds she received from the settlement with LVM made up the difference. Rose Publishing hired Tina part-time, and she also had the privilege of working part-time for the local outreach pastor at RHCC. Tina was then offered a full time position at RHCC in the communications department—now that was right up her alley! She worked on the weekly worship folder, church directory, ministry booklet, and other print design projects. Tina was also blessed with the ability to specify and set up an Apple graphics workstation to bring some of RHCC's graphic work in-house. Unfortunately, following the terrorist attacks on 9/11 RHCC suffered a reduction in giving, and the church was forced to cut Tina's hours. The church had a wonderful going away lunch and the director of ministry services gave a nice going-away speech and announced if a position ever opened up in communications, Tina would be the first woman she'd call for the job.

Tina has been blessed to travel to over twenty-two countries. The Lord has given her a great love for other cultures, and an adventurous spirit. God will use the traits He's formed in us for His glory.

*I have become all things to all **men**, that I might by all means save some. Now this I do for the gospel's sake, that I may be partaker of it with **you**.*
(1 Corinthians 9:22-23)

What ORANGE threads of character has God created you with? [187]

_____

_____

_____

_____

_____

_____

_____

_____

_____

_____

_____

_____

_____

_____

_____

_____

_____

_____

_____

_____

_____

Tina thought sexual sin wouldn't enter into the equation when dating a Christian man, especially considering the man she dated planned to serve as a missionary. Unfortunately, that simply wasn't the case (we're still human) and she once again faced her inability to set appropriate, Godly boundaries. Although they confessed their sin to the Lord and their pastors, the relationship was not restored. It was God's way of protecting Tina from marrying a man who would not "love her as Christ loves the church." We learn and grow as God chastens us, as a loving father disciplines his children. God disciplines those He loves so they might learn and "yield the peaceable fruit of righteousness."[25]

Husbands, love your wives, just as Christ also loved the church and gave Himself for her. (Ephesians 5:25)

Are there any shades of ORANGE in your life that you should not allow into your tapestry? [188]

_____

_____

_____

_____

_____

_____

_____

_____

_____

_____

_____

_____

_____

_____

Trust in the LORD with all your heart,
And lean not on your own understanding;
In all your ways acknowledge Him,
And He shall direct your paths.
(Proverbs 3:5-6)

What ORANGE threads of God's divine direction are being woven into your life tapestry right now? [189]

_____

_____

_____

_____

_____

_____

_____

_____

_____

_____

_____

_____

_____

_____

_____

_____

_____

_____

_____

_____

_____

_____

_____

_____

_____

_____

_____

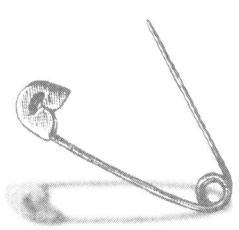

BROWN
The Fall of Pride

For the first time since Tina left her job at LVM she had to look for work outside the Christian community because the money she received from her settlement was quickly dwindling. Tina expected to be moving overseas to serve as a missionary and hadn't planned accordingly. She was quite fearful, as she hadn't yet learned to trust the Lord completely, in every aspect of her life. God had closed the door for missions and, since she had been on such a mountaintop spiritually, Tina never really allowed the Lord, through His Word, to dig down deep enough to help her completely work through her years of sexual and emotional abuse. Tina still felt vulnerable and insecure.

After going on a few interviews Tina was hired as marketing manager for United Yellow Pages (UYP), her first job back out in the world since leaving LVM, and her salvation experience. Tina lost the fifty pounds she had gained and enjoyed all the attention she received from the men at UYP, especially the owner. She started dressing more like the other women in marketing, which was rather provocative (mini-skirts). Tina thought she was simply dressing cute. As if God had transformed Tina's mind to that of a child; she was rather gullible and naïve.

While at United Yellow Pages, Tina learned of an opening in the communications department at RHCC but not from the director of ministry services who had assured Tina she would be the first person called if a position opened up. Tina applied and interviewed for the job but never heard anything even after the position was filled. Not getting the job didn't bother Tina, but not hearing anything from the RHCC either way did. Tina was disheartened by the church, disappointed by people she had looked up to as Christians.

She felt hurt and began to hold resentment toward the church and other believers there. Satan was setting the stage for a perfect storm.

Kim, one of Tina's girlfriends from high school, called and invited her to a party. Kim mentioned there would be alcohol at the party but Tina decided to go anyway. When Tina got there, not a single person was without an alcoholic beverage in their hand; everyone was drinking. Tina was tired of trying to live a perfect, sinless life. She didn't want to be a fuddy-duddy. So, that night she drank along with everyone else. Using the excuse of the church and Christians letting her down, Tina fell back into the same areas of sin the Lord had delivered her from years earlier.

Tina had been very prideful in her walk with the Lord. She thought she was "little miss super Christian" and would judge those who weren't. She recalls singing in the choir and noticing a woman always smelling of alcohol, thinking, "How dare she? She must not be a Christian." What? How dare Tina! Tina needed humbling, but had no idea what was in store for her. She had also been holding onto old patterns of trying to prove herself worthy of God's love just like she had for years in an attempt to gain her family's love and acceptance. She hadn't truly realized the depths of God's grace—the price was paid in full on Calvary. Tina didn't need to do anything to earn God's love or acceptance. He proved it by sending His Son to die. We need to recognize God's grace, and pray He allows us to not only see ourselves through His eyes of grace, but also see others in the body of Christ, who may be struggling, through those same eyes of grace.

Working at UYP, Tina was attracted to a man named Gage, who was a graphic designer there. He was creative, good looking, and gave Tina the kind of attention she hadn't received in a long time. She was torn by her attraction to him because he wasn't a Christian. Tina shared her dilemma with one of her girlfriends at church who encouraged Tina to date him anyway. She told Tina perhaps God was going to use Tina to bring Gage to salvation, since he knew she was a Christian. Tina didn't need to hear more and gave herself permission to date Gage. On some level, Tina knew her choice was wrong, but had no idea how much pain she was in store for. Gage and Tina's first date was on New Year's Eve after a conversation between the two revealed that neither of them had any plans. They began dating more and after a few months, Tina decided to tell Gage she had been celibate for nearly seven years. She told him that she was tired of trying to be good all the time. Tina fell and fell hard.

About two and a half years into her relationship with Gage, his best friends' wife, Ginger, had invited Tina to join her on a girl's night out. The plan was for Tina to meet the girls at a posh restaurant in Santa Monica. Tina rushed home from work, showered, dressed up in a tiny black dress, and headed on her way. She even stopped by the bank on the way there to make sure she had enough cash to cover dinner and drinks, not assuming everything would be paid for, as she had been told. Tina called Ginger to tell her she was on her way but there was no answer. She tried calling Ginger again and again but had no luck. Arriving at the restaurant in Santa Monica, Tina called again—still no answer. She went inside and looked everywhere, but couldn't find Ginger or the girls anywhere.

Upset and disappointed, Tina called Gage, but he didn't answer his phone. So she headed back toward home and, on the way, called her friend Kim to vent. Kim suggested Tina join her and her new boyfriend at a club in Hermosa Beach to listen to a friend's band play. Tina quickly took Kim up on the invitation. As soon as they entered the club, Tina pulled out the wad of money she had withdrawn earlier, and bought them all drinks. Tina bought drink after drink, shot after shot while she expressed her anger about the girl's night out; all the while saying she didn't normally drink so much. Kim and her boyfriend, Nathan, were both empathetic, and invited Tina to spend the night at Nathan's house so she wouldn't have to drive home. Unfortunately, Nathan and Kim got rather hot and heavy on the dance floor and ended up leaving the club without Tina. Tina wound up staying at the club while they closed the place, drinking with the bartender, who gave her a shot of Jägermeister on her way out the door.

Tina had way too much to drink and should not have been driving. She took the scenic way home, around the coast of Palos Verdes Peninsula. It was after two in the morning. After one too many drinks and not paying much attention to the road, she was pulled over by the police. They asked Tina a ton of questions and told her to get out of the car. She agreed to a field sobriety test and failed miserably. Feeling terrible for what she had done, Tina kept apologizing all the way to the police station. She was so naïve. Tina had no idea how serious driving while intoxicated is, or that she would actually end up spending the night in a Palos Verdes jail cell. It was a horrible experience for her! There she was, a woman who just a few years earlier worked at the church and was commissioned to serve as a missionary, spending the night in jail. Tina was so ashamed!

When Kim called her the next day, Tina said, "Guess where I spent the night?" Kim replied in laughter, "In jail?" When Tina said yes, Kim laughed hysterically. Tina certainly didn't find it funny. Tina called Gage, telling him what happened and how she never heard from, or met up with, the girls. Gage later told his best friend about Tina's night, and they all had a good laugh, commenting how nearly all their friends had DUIs at one time or another. They made light of the situation. No one apologized to Tina for the botched girls night out, or offered any excuse for why they never returned Tina's calls. The whole situation wasn't the least bit funny to Tina. She had no idea what she was going to do, or how much this mistake would cost her. Tina hired a lawyer since she had no idea how this worked; she had never before been in trouble with the law. The lawyer did little other than postpone the trial date for a year. Even then, Tina never did stand before a judge, the lawyer appeared for her. Over ten thousand dollars later, thirty days without driving, attending traffic school, paying off the loan she got to pay the lawyer, and seven years, the DUI is no longer on her record, praise God!

Tina was somewhat miserable at her job at UYP. She was hired as their marketing manager, but ended up as more of a glorified graphic designer, and she was bored. When one of her clients from her freelance graphic design days called her for some work he needed, she informed him she wasn't doing graphics full time any longer, but if he was ever in the market for someone full time, she would definitely be interested. Not long afterward, he called her in for an interview, and she was hired to work at Medical Air Systems (MAS). Though she had just gotten the DUI, because of Tina's honesty the owner extended a lot of grace and hired her regardless of the DUI. Fortunately, Tina's sister-in-law, Kate, worked in the area and was able to drive Tina to and from work during the month her license was suspended.

Satan used Tina's sin to keep her away from the church, away from God's word, and bound in shame and guilt. It took some time for the Lord to open Tina's eyes to the fact He still loved her, and would forgive her rebellion and sin. Although years before Tina had understood God's love, it wasn't until this time she began to fully understand God's grace. His grace doesn't give us license to sin, but His grace is available when we fully repent and put our faith and trust in the One who never gives up on us. He is the Father Tina never knew; the Father who loves her unconditionally; the One who disciplines out of love; the One who would never leave her nor forsake her.

A few months after the DUI, Tina found out the girls' night out was planned so Gage could go on a date with someone he had met over the internet. Tina also learned Gage had been lying to her from the very beginning of their relationship. Although Tina loved Gage and considered him a good friend, the fact she no longer worked at UYP made it easier for her to leave him. It was a painful, but necessary, breakup. She dated two men after Gage, both non-Christian. One was director of an art gallery in Beverly Hills; the other an Emmy award-winning television editor. Both relationships were empty, and went nowhere. Slowly, Tina came to realize a lot of the men she had dated were simply a vain attempt to gain her family's love and acceptance. She thought if someone important loved and accepted her, perhaps her family would love and accept her.

Satan knows our weak spots and, if we're not grounded in God's word and surrounded by other Christians who can help hold us accountable, we're destined to fall. Tina dated Gage for three years and, after her DUI, attended church less and less until she stopped altogether. Her life was right back where it was before she gave her life to Christ. But, this time the inner turmoil was killing her. She knew exactly what she was doing—living a disobedient, rebellious life—and deep down inside she felt miserable. She would often pray, confessing her sin, but also expressing how she didn't feel like stopping, so would plead with the Lord for a change of heart. Tina wasn't fully repentant yet, and needed the Lord to get her to a place where she would be.

God had put a few people in Tina's life He had used over and over to bring her to the place He wanted her. Just when she would be in her darkest hour, lo and behold, Tina would get an e-mail from Lynda, the wife of the senior pastor of RHCC, asking how Tina was doing. For Tina, Lynda was the personification of the love of God on earth. She never judged Tina or forgot about her, even when she was fully living in sin. Lynda knew everything, all Tina's dirty little secrets, yet she still extended an arm of grace and love; now that's a Christian! The Lord used Lynda many times throughout Tina's life to reveal His love for her and to prompt her to return to her first love—Jesus.

Little by little Tina began to attend church again and shared the details of her fall and sin with close, trusted Christian friends. Since her friends from church didn't know Tina before, they were shocked when she told them about her DUI; it was so out of character for her.

All sin is horrific in God's eyes. For this reason God the Son came to earth in human form to die. Jesus shed His blood for all sinners. He died so we could be forgiven, no matter how terrible the sin may seem. I pray the Lord will remove the scales from the eyes of all who are bound by the lie they are too bad for God to forgive. I pray they will recognize the One who paid the penalty for their sin—Jesus.

Tina understands God's grace much more now than she had in the past. He never let her go, even in her rebellious state. The Lord knows our heart. He extended grace to Tina, and drew her back to her first love—Jesus .

> *For what I am doing, I do not understand. For what I will to do, that I do not practice; but what I hate, that I do. O wretched man that I am! Who will deliver me from this body of death? I thank God—through Jesus Christ our Lord! (Romans 7:14-15, 24-25)*

What are your BROWN struggles right now? [190]

_____

_____

_____

_____

_____

_____

_____

_____

_____

_____

_____

_____

_____

_____

_____

_____

_____

_____

There's a reason why God doesn't want us to "*be unequally yoked together with unbelievers.*" Dating a man who was not a Christian was the beginning of Tina's fall. She thought she was strong enough in her Christian walk to stand against temptation. If we continue to place ourselves in vulnerable situations, the enemy is liable to gain a foothold.

Are you dating a non-Christian? What BROWN threads are being woven into your tapestry as a result? [191]

The Lord blessed Tina early in her walk as a Christian. She began working in Christian ministry within the first year she became a Christian. It wasn't long before she became puffed up and prideful. As a result she fell and fell hard. Tina was taking in solid food before her teeth came in, and she ended up choking. But God didn't leave her lying face down on the ground choking. Did she suffer the consequences for her sin? Yes. Because the Lord loves us enough to discipline us, He did Tina until she was back home safe in His arms.

But He gives more grace. Therefore He says:
"God resists the proud, But gives grace to the humble."
(James 4:6)

Are there any BROWN shades of pride in your life right now? [192]

_____
_____
_____
_____
_____
_____
_____
_____
_____
_____
_____
_____
_____
_____
_____
_____
_____
_____

In retrospect, Tina understands she may have been trying to prove herself to God; to gain His love and acceptance by doing rather than trusting in the truth that He loves her just as she is. He proved His love for her on the cross!

*For by grace you have been saved through faith, and that not of yourselves; **it is** the gift of God, not of works, lest anyone should boast."*
(Ephesians 2:8-9)

List some of the BROWN threads of grace God is weaving in your life tapestry. [193]

You can still be disappointed in the church, even serving or working in ministry, because the church and ministries are full of imperfect, emotional human beings. The only One you can truly rely on is the Lord. If you put the majority of your trust and faith in people rather than the Lord, you will always be let down and disappointed. On the other hand, if you keep your eyes on Jesus and ensure He's the reason you're serving in ministry, and attending church services, you'll never be disappointed and He will give you the ability to see people through His eyes, accepting them for who they are (and aren't).

> **It is** better to trust in the LORD
> Than to put confidence in princes.
> (Psalm 118:9)

Is God enough for you or are you looking to the BROWNS outside for fulfillment and direction? [194]

After her hours were cut at RHCC, Tina had to look for a job outside the Christian community. She feared for her future. No matter where she ended up working she was fearful of losing her job. She lacked confidence and didn't trust that God would take care of her. Her imagination would run wild with all the what-ifs. "What if I lose my job? What if I can't pay my rent? What if my family won't help me? What if the church won't help me?" She left God out of the equation.

*Now if anyone builds on this foundation **with** gold, silver, precious stones, wood, hay, straw, each one's work will become clear; for the Day will declare it, because it will be revealed by fire; and the fire will test each one's work, of what sort it is. If anyone's work which he has built on it endures, he will receive a reward. If anyone's work is burned, he will suffer loss; but he himself will be saved, yet so as through fire.*
(1 Corinthians 3:12-15)

Are there BROWN threads of worry in your life right now? [195]

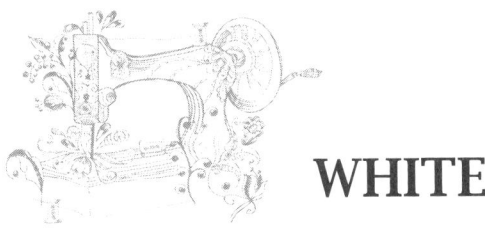

WHITE
The Beauty of the Adventure

As briefly mentioned in the Brown chapter, Tina was miserable working at United Yellow Pages. The culture was not a good one. The marketing girls were young, wild, and flirtatious, feeding the owner's ego, and sending the message it was OK for him to mix business with pleasure. Yes, once again, Tina found herself being flattered by the owner of the company she worked for. Thankfully, an old client Tina had met at church years earlier, offered her a job at the company he owned (MAS), and she happily accepted. She is happy to be working for a company that conducts business with the utmost honesty and integrity. The long, commute in LA traffic can be tough at times, but it provides Tina with much needed time for prayer and worship.

When Tina first started going to church again, she was still struggling with alcohol and her extreme craving for love and acceptance. She still felt guilty and full of shame every time she walked into the church sanctuary. One evening as she pulled into her driveway after a long hard day at work, the song "Jesus Take The Wheel" by Carrie Underwood came bursting through the speakers. Tina sat there in her car and, as the Holy Spirit touched her, tears streamed down her face. With hands in the air, palms up, in an act of complete surrender, Tina began singing, pleading with Jesus to "take the wheel." She absolutely could not stop the pattern of sin she had allowed herself to get so entangled in by her own power. Truth is, none of us has the power to live a life of obedience without the help of the Holy Spirit. Tina was, once again bound by sin and miserable. Tina met with one of the RHCC pastors, he encouraged her to visit a new group they were forming at the church called Celebrate Recovery[26] (CR). CR is a ministry designed to help those struggling with hurts, habits, and hang-ups by revealing the loving power of Jesus Christ through a recovery process. The first night Tina walked into CR she was scared to death. Tina didn't feel as though she fit in and was frightened of being judged if she were honest about her struggle with habitual sin, especially as a Christian. To the contrary, the group made Tina feel loved and accepted, even after the other women there learned of her sin. Many others in the group were struggling with similar issues of sin and were there to work through them using the Bible without judgment or condemnation.

The Lord used CR in a mighty way in Tina's life, and she was able to serve in ministry again. In full repentance, she turned away from those areas of sin and, realizing the areas in which she was weak, laid them before the Lord, knowing full well that without submitting to Him and allowing the Holy Spirit to reign in her life, she would surely fail. Tina realized she had often attempted to prove herself worthy of God's love by doing the right thing, serving in ministry, giving, and other acts. All those things are wonderful, but must not be used to prove yourself worthy or to earn God's love. Those actions should be in response to the fact He already loves us. The Lord blessed Tina a great deal through the CR ministry, and she grew when He allowed her to serve on the leadership team, leading other women who struggle with alcohol and relationship addiction through the Christ-centered twelve-step program. Tina even got to sing with the CR worship band. Tina was, once again, right where she belonged, in the arms of her loving, kind, gracious, merciful, patient Savior, and she no longer felt guilty or condemned when she set foot inside the church.

Tina started attending regular church services and even inched her way back up toward the front row. It took some time for the Lord to get it through her thick skull He still loved her even after all she had done. She was so convicted, she often questioned her salvation. She met with some of the pastors and Lynda, who the Lord used to reveal the depth of His grace by pointing her to verses which helped her gain assurance of her salvation (*Romans 8:38–39*). First of all, she would have felt no conviction and no remorse for the sin she had committed had she not truly been saved (*Hebrews 4:12*). Secondly, she would have never have come to the point of repentance had she not been saved. Finally, God would have simply let her go if she wasn't His in the first place, but He didn't. You see, her fall and her being where she is today is a perfect example of the depths of God's grace. His grace doesn't give us license to sin, but it's there when we really need it—because He loves us so much. Tina hadn't fully understood God's grace. He allowed her to fall into sin because, once again, she had a lesson to learn and He loves her enough to allow her to make terrible decisions which He uses to teach her lessons. Each time she learns a little bit more, so she hopefully won't make the same mistake again.

Allowing Him to take the wheel and drive is the key. Every time Tina tries to drive her life, which is quite often, she ends up crashing (i.e., falling into sin). Sometimes the crash is into a nice, soft embankment; sometimes into a concrete wall. Sometimes it takes days to recover from the wounds she's caused, while other wounds literally take years to recover from. Quite frankly, she's still recovering from the last big accident she caused.

In recent years the Lord has continued to weave the tapestry of Tina's life. He's added more brightly colored threads by allowing her to buy her first home. The threads of Tina's life are being stretched as she moved from the area where she grew up, to Orange County. Initially Tina felt extremely alone but, in that time of wandering in the wilderness, she sensed God wanted her all to Himself. Tina realized how often she had put people, church, and serving in ministry, above the Lord. All those things are good but if they take time away from God Himself we need to regroup. That's what He did with Tina. When she changed her focus from trying to find friends and a church to using the time alone to spend with the Lord and seek where He wanted her, the desert turned into a fresh stream of living water. It wasn't long after that realization that a friend told Tina about a new church in Irvine called Harvest OC[5] (Greg Laurie) and, after attending nine different churches since her move, the Lord landed her there. Harvest OC is a church dedicated to sharing the good news of Jesus and the Lord has allowed Tina to serve Him in the areas He has so graciously gifted her, all for His glory. Tina doesn't know what color the Lord might choose to weave in her tapestry next but she trusts that He will place it in the perfect spot, for His perfect purpose, in His perfect will, with His amazing love, for His glory and His glory alone.

Tina thanks the Lord for not letting her go; even after her outright rebellion. She thanks Him for proving, once again, how much He loves her, and for helping her realize nothing can separate her from His love.

For I am persuaded that neither death nor life, nor angels nor principalities nor powers, nor things present nor things to come, nor height nor depth, nor any other created thing, shall be able to separate us from the love of God which is in Christ Jesus our Lord. (Romans 8:38-39)

What WHITE threads in your life are being refined through the fire of God's great love? [196]

_____
_____
_____
_____
_____
_____
_____
_____
_____
_____
_____

The Lord will continue the work He began in Tina, and she knows, without a shadow of a doubt, He will be faithful to complete it.

He who has begun a good work in you
*will complete **it** until the day of Jesus Christ.*
(Philippians 1:6)

What good work has God begun in the weaving of WHITE into your tapestry? [197]

_____

_____

_____

_____

_____

_____

_____

_____

_____

_____

_____

_____

_____

_____

_____

_____

_____

_____

_____

_____

_____

_____

_____

_____

_____

"Come now, and let us reason together,"
Says the LORD, "Though your sins are like scarlet,
They shall be as white as snow; Though they are
red like crimson, They shall be as wool."
(Isaiah 1:18)

Are you aware of how WHITE God sees you through the blood of Jesus? What sins has God cleansed you of? *198/199/200*

_____

_____

_____

_____

_____

_____

_____

_____

_____

_____

_____

_____

_____

_____

_____

_____

_____

_____

_____

_____

_____

_____

_____

_____

Now may the God of peace who brought up our Lord
Jesus from the dead, that great Shepherd of the sheep,
through the blood of the everlasting covenant, make
you complete in every good work to do
His will, working in you what is well pleasing
in His sight, through Jesus Christ,
*to whom **be** glory forever and ever.*
Amen. (Hebrews 13:20-21)

What WHITE fingerprints of God can you see working in your life? [201]

_____

_____

_____

_____

_____

_____

_____

_____

_____

_____

_____

_____

_____

_____

_____

_____

_____

_____

_____

_____

Rejoice in the Lord always.
Again I will say, rejoice!
(Philippians 4:4)

What WHITE reasons for rejoicing has the Lord given you? [202]

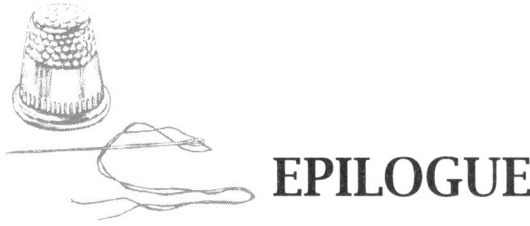

EPILOGUE
Still Growing after All These Years

Tina is still growing in the grace and knowledge of our Lord. She still gets lonely at times. She is still grieved when something tragic happens, or someone close to her gets ill. She's still impatient on the freeway during her commute. She still sometimes focuses on her own desires. She's still Tina. She doesn't know if she'll ever get married, but she trusts that if God has someone out there for her, He will orchestrate a way for them to meet or He will remove her desire for marriage.

Tina doesn't know what's going to happen tomorrow but she trusts whatever does happen, God is in control. She doesn't know how the Lord will use her and the gifts and abilities He has so graciously bestowed upon her. Tina prays that however she uses those gifts and abilities will glorify the Lord. She doesn't know if she will ever have complete patience, but she prays for God's grace and guidance for such patience. Tina knows when she sins, God still loves her, and will teach her and give her strength to stand against temptation. She doesn't know who around her will come to faith in Christ and who won't, but Tina prays for them and trusts God will reach those whom He has already chosen, and He will use her, if He so chooses, to deliver directions to the lost.

And that, dear ones,
is what I pray for all who read this.

The truth is, if you're not living in a right relationship with God, you're not really living as you were created to live. People around you will disappoint and hurt you. Circumstances will affect your life and the way you live it, negatively and positively. When you encounter serious illness, injury, or loss of a loved one, you will more than likely crumble under the weight and depth of despair. Money will control you. Who you choose to hang out with, and how many friends you have or don't have, will have an influence on how acceptable you believe yourself to be. What you look like on the outside will shape how you feel on the inside. If you were abandoned by a parent or loved one, other relationships will be lived in fear and insecurity. If you live to please others you will never find peace. If you live to please yourself, you will never find joy. Only through having a right relationship with the One who created you—almighty God—will you find fulfillment, peace, and joy.

You may be asking yourself, "Do I have a right relationship with God? How can I know whether or not I do?" The Bible says all have sinned and fall short of the glory of God.[27] Included in that "all" is you. Many of us think if we're good enough we'll go to heaven. But let me ask you something . . . have you ever told a lie, even once, even a tiny little white lie? If you have, you've broken God's law and committed a sin, as the Bible states "*You shall not bear false witness against your neighbor" (Exodus 20:16)*. Have you ever wished you had something someone else had: their house, their riches, their car, their designer clothes, their popularity, their looks? If you have, you've sinned—the Bible says "*You shall not covet your neighbor's house; you shall not covet your neighbor's wife, nor his male servant, nor his female servant, nor his ox, nor his donkey, nor anything that is your neighbor's" (Exodus 20:17).*

Even if you've broken one of God's laws only one time, and even if it was in the past, you're still guilty of breaking His law (sin), and are deserving of the punishment required for breaking the law, which is death and eternity in hell, forever separated from the God who loves you. Some take hell lightly, thinking, "Good, I can spend time with friends partying for all eternity." But hell is certainly no party. Imagine the worst pain you've ever experienced, physical or emotional, and multiply by ten billion, and you still don't scratch the surface of the pain and torment of hell. Worse, it doesn't last a lifetime, or even ten lifetimes; it lasts for all of eternity—a length of time we can't even begin to fathom. Picture the grains of sand making up the Sahara desert. Imagine how many grains of sand it would take to cover the earth. Now imagine how many grains of sand it would take cover every single planet in the universe (some of which have yet to be discovered). Imagine how long it would take for each and every one of those tiny grains of sand to trickle through an hourglass; that doesn't even begin to approach a millionth of a second in relationship to eternity. Do you really want to spend eternity in such pain and torment?

So you believe in a loving God who will forgive you and allow you to enter heaven when you die. If that's the case, the same god would allow everyone to enter heaven when they die, including rapists and murderers who never admitted guilt for their crime or felt sorrow for what they did. If someone brutally murdered the person closest to you, the one you love more than anything, would you want to spend eternity with that murderer? Would God be a loving god if He allowed an unrepentant, guilty murderer into heaven? If God is loving and just, He cannot allow the guilty to enter into His presence in heaven. The truth is the one guilty of committing the crime must pay the just punishment for that crime (do the crime, spend the time). Well, we are all deserving of punishment since we have all committed a crime against God (sin). That punishment is death; we're all deserving of the death penalty. The Bible says, *"without shedding of blood there is no remission"* (*Hebrews 9:22*).

But there is HOPE, dear friend. God loves YOU! He loves you so much He sent His only begotten Son to pay the penalty for your sin and set you free. Jesus—God in the flesh—came to this earth in the form of a man, hung on a cross and shed His blood for the remission (release from a debt, penalty, or obligation) of our sin, and rose from the dead three days later, victorious. But you have to accept and receive the gift God sent His Son to die to give you (the payment made for our crime), otherwise you still stand guilty before

Him, deserving of punishment. If you have never admitted your guilt (sin), turned away from your crime (repentance), accepted the price God paid, and put your faith and trust in Jesus, I urge you to do so. Spend time in God's word (the Bible—the way He has chosen to speak to us), in prayer (the way we talk to God), in fellowship with other believers (church—the way we are encouraged and strengthened), and share this wonderful news with those around you.

A restored relationship with the God who created you, the One who loves you more than anyone on earth ever could, is the first step toward understanding the various colors He's weaving together in the tapestry of your life. Allow Him to speak to you through His Word (the Bible), and begin the healing process. He will lead you on an adventure you will never regret taking. He will give you the strength to carry on when you approach those deep, dark valleys. And, when you reach the other side, He will bless you in ways you would have never imagined had it not been for those dark, dreary, colors making your own tapestry so very beautiful.

Why not record your response in a prayer to the One who created you; almighty God.

*Therefore, if anyone is in Christ, **he is** a new creation; old things have passed away; behold, all things have become new.*
(2 Corinthians 5:17)

If you've put your faith and trust in Jesus as Lord and Savior of your life, you are a new creation.

_____
_____
_____
_____
_____
_____
_____
_____
_____
_____
_____
_____
_____
_____
_____
_____
_____
_____
_____
_____
_____
_____
_____
_____
_____
_____
_____
_____
_____
_____

ROMAN ROAD to SALVATION

Romans 3:10
There is none righteous, no, not one;

Romans 3:23
for all have sinned and fall short of the glory of God,

Romans 5:12
Therefore, just as through one man sin entered the world, and death through sin, and thus death spread to all men, because all sinned

Romans 6:23
*For the wages of sin **is** death, but the free gift of God **is** eternal life in Christ Jesus our Lord.*

Romans 5:8
But God demonstrates His own love toward us, in that while we were still sinners, Christ died for us.

Romans 10:9-10
if you confess with your mouth Jesus as Lord, and believe in your heart that God raised Him from the dead, you will be saved; for with the heart a person believes, resulting in righteousness, and with the mouth he confesses, resulting in salvation.

Romans 10:13
for Whoever will call on the name of the LORD will be saved.

TAPESTRY LESSONS
A Message from Teri

What lessons has God taught Tina while He's been so intricately weaving her tapestry . . . a tapestry that, while comprised of many bright and beautiful, bland and bleak, and dark and dreary colors, has yet to be fully completed? Upon the following pages lie but a few the Lord has placed upon my heart to share with you. My hope and prayer is the Lord might use these threads to inspire, encourage, and give you strength in the midst of darkness, to stand firm and remember God is weaving your life into something beautiful He will reveal on the day of completion (*James 1:2-4*).

I pray these will help you fully realize just how much God loves you. Open in prayer as you open His word and allow Him to speak into your heart.

Now may our Lord Jesus Christ Himself,
and our God and Father, who has loved us
*and given **us** everlasting consolation*
and good hope by grace,
comfort your hearts and establish you
in every good word and work."
(2 Thessalonians 2:16-17)

Now may the God of hope fill you with all joy
and peace in believing, that you may abound
in hope by the power of the Holy Spirit.
(Romans 15:13)

> ## No matter how invisible you may sometimes feel, you can rest in the fact that God truly sees you.

Read *Genesis 16*

Abram and Sarai doubted God's promise that they would conceive a child. So Sarai took Hagar, her maid, and gave her to her husband Abram to be his wife and she conceived. But when Sarai saw that she had conceived, Hagar became despised in her eyes. Sarai twisted the story as she told Abram that she herself was despised by Hagar. Abram left the decision up to his wife and, as a result, Sarai dealt harshly with Hagar and Hagar fled from Sarai's presence.

Think about how Hagar must have felt pregnant and alone in the wilderness. But God didn't leave her in that state of despair. He saw her there. He heard her affliction. He instructed Hagar to return to Sarai and promised He would "*multiply her descendents.*" As a result, Hagar called the name of the LORD who spoke to her, "*You-Are-the-God-Who-Sees.*"

You are not invisible to God.

He knows your every thought. He knows your every dream. He knows your every sorrow. So the next time you're tempted to think you don't matter—that no one cares—look up; God cares!

List some of the ways God sees you.

_____

_____

_____

_____

_____

_____

_____

_____

The Lord looks from heaven; He <u>sees</u> all the
sons of men. From the place of His dwelling
He looks On all the inhabitants of the earth;
He fashions their hearts individually;
He considers all their works.
(Psalm 33:13-15; emphasis mine)

You are beautiful in God's eyes.

List some of the beautiful ways in which the Bible says God
sees you and the attributes He's created in you.

_____

_____

_____

_____

_____

_____

_____

_____

_____

_____

_____

_____

_____

_____

_____

_____

_____

_____

_____

_____

_____

_____

_____

_____

You are precious in God's sight.

Read *Ephesians 1:3-14*

God actually choses those He desires to call His children. He adopted Tina into His family. The same God who created heaven and earth hand picks His children. He desires to call us out of darkness and brings us into His marvelous light.

God doesn't just choose the beautiful people; although we are beautiful in His eyes. God doesn't just choose the most intelligent, or those who are musically creative or gifted in some other way. He created us to be exactly who we are, and we are precious to Him.

God wants to call you His child.

God loves you so much He sent His Son to die so you could become His child. Let Him adopt you. Put your faith in Jesus and run into your Daddy's arms. He's waiting for you with open arms.

What does it say in Ephesians about God's role in salvation? What does that mean to you?

See also *John 1:10-13; Romans 8:12-17; Galatians 3:26-29; 1 Peter 2:9-10;* and *1 John 3:1-3*

No matter what, if you are a child of God, He will <u>never</u> abandon you.

Read *Deuteronomy 31:6*

In the beginning of Tina's Christian walk she thought if she sinned God would leave her just like her biological dad did. But quite the contrary, our Lord is no absentee Father.

God will never leave you nor forsake you.

I know from my own personal experience that even when I fall into sin, God is right there waiting for me. He's got an outstretched arm waiting for me to reach up and grab. He's waiting for me to get up, dust myself off, put my hand in His, and allow Him to help me walk in a straight line so I won't lose my balance and fall. We need not fear He will ever leave us, but keep our eyes upon the Father who loves us so much that He gave His only begotten Son. Allow Him to help you walk and He will never leave your side.

In what ways are you allowing the Lord to help you walk? Are you trusting God to stick by you, even in times you're weak?

_____

_____

_____

_____

_____

_____

_____

_____

_____

_____

_____

_____

See also *Joshua 1:5; Romans 8:31-39; Hebrews 13:5-6;* and *1 John 1:8-10.*

Sex does not equate to love, and having sex outside of marriage affects your innermost being—your soul.

Read *1 Corinthians 6:15-20*

Having sex outside of marriage is harmless, right? No! God's word clearly speaks against it, but why? Having sex not only leaves one vulnerable to emotional pain and suffering, but physical suffering as well. Sexual promiscuity opens the door for sexually transmitted diseases and unplanned pregnancy. Don't get me wrong, God created man and woman and He created sex. But He also set clear boundaries that sex is to be enjoyed within the confines of marriage.

But why? Having sex brings two people together in the most intimate sense. The Bible states the two actually become as one flesh. So what happens when the two are separated? The flesh is actually split apart. If you lose a limb is your body still whole? No. It's been damaged and will never fully regain the strength and ability it once had. Our heavenly Father does not want to see us suffer, which is precisely why He set such boundaries.

God loves you!

God loves you and He wants to protect you from the unnecessary pain and suffering that is so often caused by sexual promiscuity.

What does 1 Corinthians 6:15-20 say about your body?

_____

_____

_____

_____

_____

_____

See also *1 Thessalonians 4:1-8* and *2 Timothy 2:22.*

> ## What you look like on the outside, the way you dress, and how much you weigh do not define your value.

Read *Psalm 139:13-16*

God created you as an individual. He knitted you together in your mother's womb. Even before you were born God was planning your existence. He knows every individual cell in your body. You are fearfully and wonderfully made! Nothing in a person's outward appearance impresses God. God looks upon the inner beauty, the beauty of one's heart.

You are beautiful in the eyes of God and are of great value to Him.

Did you know that God numbers the very hairs upon your head? God doesn't forget even one tiny sparrow. He will certainly not forget you. You are of much more value to Him than the sparrows He cares for.

How does knowing that God, creator of heaven and earth, sees you as beautiful, change the way you view yourself?

_____
_____
_____
_____
_____
_____
_____
_____
_____
_____
_____
_____

See also *1 Samuel 16:7; Matthew 10:30-31; Luke 12:6-7; Ephesians 2:10;* and *1 Peter 3:3-4.*

Life isn't always easy but, know this; times of trouble and despair are temporary.

Read *Psalm 34* **and** *Hebrews 10:19-25*

God hears your cries. He knows what you're going through right now. Allow Him into the wilderness of your despair. The Lord is near to those who have a broken heart.

There is always hope!

Have you cried out to God in the midst of your pain and suffering? Jesus understands perfectly. Think about the pain and suffering He endured for your salvation. List some of the ways God is with you in your trials.

See also *Psalm 18:6; Luke 11:9* and *Romans 8:18.*

<u>All</u> life is precious to God.

Read *Psalm 23:1-4*

Your life is precious to God. Are you troubled? Are you in despair? Do you feel as though no one cares what you're going through right now? Cry out to God, He will hear you. Allow Him to speak to you through His word, the Bible. God can bring peace to your soul. He loves you and desires to give you life abundant.

Your life is precious to God.

What does Psalm 23 say about the way God is with you, even in times of darkness when it doesn't "feel" like He is.

_____

_____

_____

_____

_____

_____

_____

_____

_____

_____

_____

_____

_____

_____

_____

_____

_____

_____

See also *Psalm 46:1-2.*

> **We need not concern ourselves with the lives of others but focus on the truth that God is in control always, at all times.**

Read *Psalm 34:7-8* and *James 4:13-15*

The creator of the heavens and the earth, the One who created you, is in control. You can trust Him with your life and the lives of others. Just as Tina need not concern herself with wondering whether her dad is alive or dead, you need not focus on what others are up to. But rather focus on the One who created you.

God is in control!

Are you focusing on the lives of others or what's going on around you more than you are the Lord? What do Psalm 34:7-8, Proverbs 3:1-6 and James 4:13-15 say about in whom we should place our trust?

_____

_____

_____

_____

_____

_____

_____

_____

_____

_____

_____

_____

_____

_____

See also *Proverbs 3:1-6* and *Matthew 5:43-48*.

Seeking love and acceptance from others will leave you empty. *True* **love and acceptance can only be found in Christ.**

Read *John 12:42-50*

Nearly everything Tina did in life before she knew Jesus was an attempt to gain love and acceptance from others. The art classes she took in school, the pictures she painted, the pottery she made. Everything she created with a mindset of gaining love and attention from others. And then there were the relationships she had with men. She so deeply wanted to be loved, she dated men to try to fill that deep void she felt within her heart.

Only God can fill the love void.

Are you trying to fill a void in your heart with people, things, alcohol, work, hobbies or anything else? Have you asked Jesus to take over? Have you and surrendered your <u>entire</u> life over to Him so He can fill that void?

_____

_____

_____

_____

_____

_____

_____

_____

_____

_____

_____

_____

_____

_____

See also *Proverbs 29:25-26; Romans 10:9-13;* and *2 Peter 3:9.*

165

> **Repentance isn't a one-time deal. We must repent and confess daily for whatever sins we may have committed, and seek to live an obedient life as we continue growing in the grace and knowledge of our Lord.**

Read *John 3:16-21; Ephesians 2:1-10;* and *1 John 1:1-10*

Being a perfectionist and one who so desperately yearned for love and acceptance, Tina used to imagine God getting angry and disappointed with her when she would make a mistake. She didn't fully understand His grace.

On the other hand, there are many who claim to be Christians, but you would never know it by looking at their lives. They live just as they did before they prayed to receive Jesus into their hearts.

The Bible clearly states that keeping God's commandments is one way we can know we love the Lord. But God isn't angry or disappointed in us when we sin. He wants us to go to Him, confess our sin, and repent. He's ready and waiting to forgive us.

We are washed clean through the blood of Jesus.

Have you been trying to earn God's love? How can you be sure He loves and accepts you?

_____

_____

_____

_____

_____

_____

_____

_____

See also *Psalm 51:1-13; Matthew 10:37-39;* and *1 John 2:1-6.*

The realization of the love of God compels us to live a life holy and acceptable to Him. Not only that, He gives us a helper, the Holy Spirit, who enables us to do just that—live a life pleasing to God.

Does the way you're living your life reflect your love for God?

_____
_____
_____
_____
_____
_____
_____
_____
_____
_____
_____
_____
_____
_____
_____
_____
_____
_____
_____
_____
_____
_____

See also *John 14:15-21, 15:9-10; Romans 5:8; 2 Corinthians 5:9-15;* and *1 John 2:1-11.*

> ## The Lord can give you strength in the midst of trials. He can give you comfort in the midst of suffering.

Read *Philippians 4:13* **and** *2 Corinthians 1:3-5*

If you've made it this far through the THREADS the Lord has so skillfully woven in Tina's life, you are well aware that she lost many loved ones. I am not going to minimize the fact that it is painful when someone you love dies. The pain is never completely gone. It often resurfaces on birthdays and holidays which bring back memories. Tears still fall. But this I know: God never intended us to have to bear such pain alone. Death is a result of sin and rebellion. It hurts. But God is right there beside you to uphold you in your time of pain and loss. He understands your pain. He watched His one and only Son being brutally beaten and nailed to a cross before gasping His last breath upon this earth. Oh, how it must have grieved the Father to witness the death of His Son. But what a glorious victory was won when Jesus rose from the grave.

God wants to be your comforter.

To whom should you turn for comfort and strength? Why?

_____

_____

_____

_____

_____

_____

_____

_____

_____

_____

See also *Ephesians 3:16. 6:10;* and *Colossians 1:11.*

> **God will get you through this. He can and even turn your time of suffering around and use you to encourage others.**

Read *Romans 8:18–30* and *2 Corinthians 1:3-4*

After a time of healing and restoration, the Lord graciously allows us to encourage others in their time of suffering. I'm not going to minimize the fact that times of trial and tribulation are difficult and painful. But we have a Savior who gives us hope in the midst of our suffering. Not only that, He can take tragedy and suffering and use it for good by placing us in the rignt place at the right time to allow us to be an encouragement to someone else who is going through a similar trial.

All things work together for good.

Have you noticed the Lord placing you among others who are going through what you have gone through? How might He use you to encourage and comfort them?

_____
_____
_____
_____
_____
_____
_____
_____
_____
_____
_____
_____

See also *Romans 5:1-6; 2 Corinthians 4:7-18, 9:10-23; 1 Thessalonians 4:13-14;* and *Revelation 21:4.*

God loves you unconditionally. No one on this earth can love you the way He does.

Read *1 Corinthians 13:4-7*

Is the person closest to you <u>always</u> patient and kind to you? Are they ever jealous or envious of you in any way, shape or form? Does this person ever brag or talk about what they've accomplished, or show off a new gadget, car, or outfit? Are they <u>always</u> polite? Are they <u>always</u> looking out for others before themselves? Do they ever get angry for something unrelated to sin against God? Do they <u>always</u> tell the truth, even when it might hurt someone's feelings?

No one loves you like God loves you.

What are some of the ways God's love is different from the love of humanity?

_____

_____

_____

_____

_____

_____

_____

_____

_____

_____

_____

_____

_____

_____

_____

See also *John 3:16-17; Romans 5:8; Ephesians 2:4-5;* and *1 John 4:9-10*

> ### There's nothing you can do to earn God's love. It's a free gift to those who accept it.

Read *Ephesians 2:1-10*

People are fickle and wishy washy. No matter how hard we try we don't have the ability to love unconditionally. Simply take an honest look at yourself in light of *1 Corinthians 13:4-7*. There's not a single thing we can do to earn God's love. God is rich in mercy and loves us greatly. He sent His Son to die to prove His love for us.

We can't earn God's love.

He loves us already. We need simply respond to that love by accepting the gift He gave us on the cross and putting our faith and trust in Jesus, who alone can save.

List some of the attibutes of God's love.

_____

_____

_____

_____

_____

_____

_____

_____

_____

_____

_____

_____

_____

_____

See also *Matthew 10:37-39; John 3:16; Romans 5:6-8;* and *1 Corinthians 13:4-7.*

Nothing can separate you from the love of God.

Read Romans 8:35, 37-39

Nothing, good nor bad, can separate us from the love of God which is in Christ Jesus. No matter what you may be going through, how far you may have fallen, or how distant you may 'feel' from God. Neither the fear of death nor the hope of life; no distance, high or low, no creature, not the past, present or future... NOTHING. God's love is the same yesterday, today and tomorrow. His love never changes.

God's love for you will never change.

Do you ever worry that God's love for you may change? List some of the reasons, according to God's word, you need not worry that anything will change God's mind toward you.

_____

_____

_____

_____

_____

_____

_____

_____

_____

_____

_____

_____

_____

_____

_____

See also *Isaiah 40:28; John 10:27-30; 1 John 4:8-10; James 1:17;* and *Hebrews 13:8;* and *Revelation 1:8*

It's OK to say no every once in a while. Setting appropriate, God-directed boundaries helps us keep the good in and the bad out.

Read *Matthew 10:11-16* and *Colossians 4:5-6*

Being raised without appropriate boundaries, Tina had difficulty understanding exactly what a boundary was. Knowing how to set appropriate boundaries is important. She had difficulty knowing when to say no and when not to. Tina does't like confrontation and wanted to live in peace with everyone, no matter the circumstances.

We need not allow others to hurt us or influence us to sin. Through God's word we can gain the discernment and strength we need to know when to say no.

God can give you the strength and wisdom to know when it's appropriate to say no.

What is God revealing to you, through His word, about boundaries?

_____

_____

_____

_____

_____

_____

_____

_____

_____

_____

_____

_____

_____

_____

See also *Psalm 37:30-31, 71:12-21; Proverbs 25:11-12; Mark 9:42; James 4:1-6;* and *Romans 12:19-21*

Making decisions in an attempt to gain the approval of man can be harmful to your health; spiritually and physically.

Read *Proverbs 29:25* **and** *Galatians 1:10*

Many of Tina's decisions were driven by her extreme desire to gain the approval of those around her. She was living in constant fear of rejection. The Bible tells us put our trust and dependence on God, not man. He already loves and accepts you. He proved it on the cross.

Fear God, not man.
God accepts you just the way you are.

What drives your decisions? List the reasons for trusting God more than man.

_____

_____

_____

_____

_____

_____

_____

_____

_____

_____

_____

_____

_____

_____

_____

See also *Psalm 118:8; John 5:44, 12:43; Ephesians 1:3-6; 1 Thessalonians 2:4-6;* and *1 John 3:1-3*

> **God wants to be your comfort in times of trouble. He understands your pain better than anyone. He desires to be your strength and give you rest.**

Read *Psalm 46:1-11* and *Matthew 11:28-30*

If you've recently lost a loved one, first of all I want to say I am so sorry for your loss. You that you are not alone in midst of your sorrow. Cry out to God; He is there waiting to put His loving arms around you. He wants to be your refuge and your strength.

God can comfort you in times of trouble.

What instructions does God give us in *Matthew 11:28-30* that will help you in times of trouble? How can you put it into practice?

_____

_____

_____

_____

_____

_____

_____

_____

_____

_____

_____

_____

_____

See also *Galatians 5:1* and *Hebrews 4:14–16.*

> **We have a great God of mercy who wants to give you hope even in the midst of sorrow. He wants to give you joy even in the midst of trials.**

Read *Romans 5:1-5* and *1 Peter 1:3-12*

God understands your sorrow. He longs to give you a living hope through the resurrection of Jesus Christ from the dead. He wants you to give you the ability to rejoice in the midst of trials.

Because of God's great love, we can have peace in the midst of sorrow.

What can trials and tribulations produce in us when we entrust our lives to Jesus?

_____

_____

_____

_____

_____

_____

_____

_____

_____

_____

_____

_____

_____

_____

_____

See also *Psalm 95:1-7* and *James 1:2-5.*

> It is often through times of sorrow and despair we grow closer to God. It is in the dark times He reveals His loving character in new, significant, life-changing ways.

Read *John 14:25-28* and *16:33*

As Christians, we're not promised a pain-free, sorrow-free, trouble-free life; quite the opposite. Before His crucifixion Jesus told His disciples that they would have tribulation. Jesus was telling them they would experience pressure, persecution, trouble, and distress in this world. But even in all the trials and tribulations we may experience on earth, in Christ we can have peace because He has overcome the world! Jesus doesn't leave us all alone in the midst of the dark and difficult times. He promises a Helper, the Holy Spirit, sent by the Father in Jesus' name.

In times of darkness, draw close to God.

Who is there to help us in the middle of suffering, trouble, difficulties and persecution?

_____
_____
_____
_____
_____
_____
_____
_____
_____
_____
_____

See also *Psalm 33:20-22; 1 Thessalonians 4:13-14;* and *Revelation 21:4*

God is saddened when you're hurt, abused or taken advantage of. Put on the full armor of God and stand in strength.

Read *Mark 9:42-50* and *Ephesians 6:10-18*

You are important to God. It saddens Him when you allow yourself to be taken advantage of. It hurts Him when you hurt. Almighty God, the One who created you, desires to be your protector and your strength. He can give you the boldness and wisdom to say "no" when you need to. Don't allow yourself to be treated in an unworthy manner. Put on the full armor of God and stand in His strength.

God can give you strength. Stand upon the promises of God; His word is our strength.

List the pieces of armor and the attibutes of each piece. How can putting on the full armor of God help you face the battle?

_____

_____

_____

_____

_____

_____

_____

_____

_____

_____

_____

_____

_____

_____

See also *Luke 14:34-35; 1 Corintians 9:6-11;* and *Philippians 4:13*

God wants to give you joy and freedom by giving you the ability to forgive those who have sinned against you.

Read *Matthew 6:12, 18:23-35*; and *Mark 11:25-26*.

Don't allow unforgiveness to steal the inner peace Jesus died to provide. Holding on to unforgiveness causes our hearts to be bitter and affects our communication with God. God will not hear our prayers unless we also show ourselves ready to grant forgiveness. If we are harder than iron in this regard, Christ's exhortation ought to soften us. God will take care of those who have offended us.

Our forgiving God calls us to forgive.

Are you holding any unforgiveness in your heart? List the people God is urging you to forgive and ask Him to give you the ability to fully forgive them.

_____

_____

_____

_____

_____

_____

_____

_____

_____

_____

_____

_____

See also *Matthew 5:43-48; Luke 17:1-4; Ephesians 4:32;* and *Colossians 3:12-17*

The God who created the heavens and the earth planned your birth before time began. You are of great value to Him.

Read *Psalm 139; Matthew 10:29-31;* and *Luke 12:6-7.*

You are of great value to God. He planned your birth before the world began. Every single hair on your head is numbered. He knows you, inside and out, better than you know yourself and He loves you anyway. He sent His Son to die to prove it to you. He has a plan for your life.

God values you more than you could even imagine; more than anyone else ever could.

List some of the ways God values you according to His word.

_____

_____

_____

_____

_____

_____

_____

_____

_____

_____

_____

_____

_____

_____

_____

_____

_____

See also *Luke 12:6-7; Romans 8:29; 2 Corinthians 4:6-10;* and *1 Peter 1:2-4*

Are you creative? Thank the Lord, Creator of all, for such a special gift.

Read *Ephesians 2:1-10*

God is the most creative, amazing artist ever! Just look how He paints the sky when the storm clouds subside and the sun breaks through, producing a beautiful rainbow. Has the Lord has given you an eye to look at things differently than others? Praise God for His awesome creativity and then share that view with others.

It is a blessing to be creative.

Has the God of all creation given you the gift of creativity? How might He use you to help others see the beauty of His creation?

See also *Exodus 31:1-5;* and *1 Corinthians 12:4-11*

Are you using the gifts God has given you to serve and glorify Him?

Read *Colossians 3:23-24* and *James 1:16-18*

God is the one who formed Tina with a heart of creativity. We can do absolutely nothing of eternal worth apart from the God who created us. The artwork Tina creates has changed, from darkness to light. It should be our desire, by the grace of God, to lift the soul of man toward heaven, and illuminate in new ways the multi-faceted beauty of God's holiness, power, and grace.[28]

Every good and perfect gift is from above. We are blessed by God to be a blessing to others, and live to glorify our Creator.

How are you using the gifts God has given you for His glory?

_____

_____

_____

_____

_____

_____

_____

_____

_____

_____

_____

_____

_____

_____

_____

See also *Psalm 29:1-2, 100:1-3;* and *Philippians 4:8.*

Reading books or watching movies and television shows that promote witchcraft, sorcery, vampires, and the like isn't harmless, but can leads down a dark road of deception, depression, and desolation.

Read *Matthew 6:22-23; Acts 26:18* and *Colossians 1:13-17*
If you are a Christian, God has delivered you from the power of darkness and conveyed you into the kingdom of the Son of His love—Jesus. We need to be careful about what we watch for *"The lamp of the body is the eye."* There is no need to trust anything or anyone but God with your future.

Jesus, who is the image of the invisible God, Creator of heaven and earth, is our deliverer.

Are you allowing darkness into your life? Take inventory; make a list of the things that may be dimming the light of Christ in you. Pray for God's help to keep away from those things and run to the One who died to deliver you from *the power of Satan to God.*

_____

_____

_____

_____

_____

_____

_____

_____

_____

_____

_____

_____

_____

See also *Luke 11:33-35; Romans 10:8-10;* and *1 John 3:1-9.*

Seemingly harmless things, such as reading your horoscope, using an Ouija board, going to palm readers, mediums, or fortune tellers leads to nothing but confusion and delusion about the future.

Read *Deuteronomy 18:10-12* and *Proverbs 3:5-6*

Things such as witchcraft, sorcery, consulting mediums, spiritists, and the like are an *"abomination to the LORD."* These things are dangerous. They're deceptive and only lead to darkness and confusion. It's important to steer clear of such influences. The only One we are to look to for insight is God. He is the only one who knows our future. Any other source of guidance, information, or revelation is to be rejected outright.[29]

God is in complete control and can be trusted with our future.

Are you looking to things other than God for your future? Read *1 John 4:1-6* how can you tell if a 'spirit' is from God or not?

_____

_____

_____

_____

_____

_____

_____

_____

_____

_____

_____

_____

See also *Jeremiah 29:11* and *1 Corinthians 12:3.*

The love of God compells us to repent and we are restored through the cross of Jesus Christ.

Read *2 Corinthians 7:9-11* and *2 Peter 3:8-9*

God desires all to be saved. He is patient toward us and is not willing that any should perish but that all should come to repentance. Are you stuck in sin right now? Cry out to God, He can give you the ability and desire to turn away from that sin and restore you.

God is patient in His love.

Are you stuck in an addiciton or habitual sin? Cry out to God; He can give you the strength and ability to walk away from it.

_____

_____

_____

_____

_____

_____

_____

_____

_____

_____

_____

_____

_____

_____

_____

_____

See also *Psalm 51:1-13; 1 Timothy 2:3-4; James 4:7-8* and *Revelation 2:4-5.*

Rejoice! Because of the cross of Christ, your sins are forgiven. God doesn't see your sin through the blood of Jesus. He has removed your sins as the east is from the west.

Read *Psalm 103:11-13; Ephesians 2:1-13;* **and** *1 John 1:7*

Our sins were nailed to the cross of Christ, once for all. The blood of Jesus cleanses us of sin. Through the acceptance of the gift that Jesus died to give us we are accepted by almighty God.

The blood of Jesus cleanses us from sin.

Have you fully accepted the gift Jesus died to give you? Have you been cleansed through the blood of Jesus?

_____

_____

_____

_____

_____

_____

_____

_____

_____

_____

_____

_____

_____

_____

_____

_____

_____

See also *Psalm 86:4-5;* and *1 John 5:1-10.*

Are you adventurous? Embrace the adventurous spirit the Lord has given you, and trust that He will use the traits He's formed in you for His glory.

Read *Matthew 28:18-20* **and** *1 Corinthians 9:19-23*

It takes a certain sense of adventure to go tell others about how God sent His own Son to die for them. You have to be bold to tell a complete and total stranger that there's only one way to heaven—Jesus!

We are all called to share the good news of Jesus, whether it's to your next-door neighbor or across the ocean. God can give you the power and boldness to do so. The results are up to Him so there's no pressure whatsoever. Jesus is the One who saves, not us, not our wise words or the way we deliver the gospel, as long as it's the gospel we share.

The love of Christ compels us to share the good news with the world.

Are there people in your life who need to hear the good news of Jesus? List them here. Pray for opportunities, boldness and wisdom and watch for God's perfect timing to share.

_____

_____

_____

_____

_____

_____

_____

_____

_____

_____

See also *Acts 1:8* and *2 Corinthians 5:14-15.*

God disciplines His children in love and mercy, not in anger.

Read *Hebrews 12:3-11* and *Revelation 3:19*

Tina used to picture God large and in charge, looking down just waiting for her to make a mistake so He could punish her. She thought He would get angry at her for any little thing, just like her dad did. She was afraid of God. Her parents didn't always discipline her properly. They didn't always punish her at the right time for the right reason. But that's not God!

God disciplines us solely out of love, and not anger. He does it so we won't get hurt. Like a curious child whose loving father grabs their hand away from a fire just in the nick of time, so is our God. We can trust in God's amazing grace.

For whom the LORD loves He corrects.

Is there sin in your life you have yet to turn away from? It's only a matter of time before your loving heavenly Father brings discipline to pull you back into His ever-loving arms.

_____

_____

_____

_____

_____

_____

_____

_____

_____

_____

_____

_____

See also *Psalm 103:8-13* and *Proverbs 3:11-12.*

God can give you strength to live according to His will. Ask Him to give you wisdom and direction in your Christian walk.

Read *1 Corinthians 10:12-13* and *2 Timothy 3:16-17*.

Living in this world can be tough as a Christian. Sinful influences surround us. That's why it is so important to spend time in God's word, the Bible; it is there we find the strength to stand. The Lord wants to help you in your walk as a Christian but you must seek guidance through prayer and reading the Bible to find wisdom and direction from God.

God speaks through His word—the Bible.

Are you struggling in your Christian walk? Are you spending time in God's word every day? Are you putting yourself in tempting situations? How can you keep yourself from temptation?

_____

_____

_____

_____

_____

_____

_____

_____

_____

_____

_____

_____

_____

_____

_____

See also *Psalm 19:7-10, 119:97-105; Proverbs 3:5-6; Philippians 4:13;* and *Hebrews 4:12*

Even if you fail God won't leave you. He's ready and waiting with open arms to receive you back home.

Read *Psalm 27:7-10; Luke 15:1-31* and *Hebrews 13:5-6*

Tina used to imagine God as a man just like her biological dad. She thought He would leave her just like her dad did. She thought nothing she did was good enough and that, no matter how hard she tried, He would never really love her enough to stick around. That's not our God! He Himself has promised He will never leave us.

God will NEVER leave you nor forsake you. His grace is sufficient; His strength is made perfect in our weakness.

Do you know that God will never abandon you? Is there anything in your past that might be keeping you from fully accepting that?

_____

_____

_____

_____

_____

_____

_____

_____

_____

_____

_____

_____

_____

See also *Joshua 1:5; Psalm 86:3-15; Romans 7:13-25;* and *2 Corinthians 12:8-10.*

Dating a non-Christian doesn't work no matter how hard you may try.

Read *2 Corinthians 6:14-18* **and** *James 4:4*

There's a good reason why God doesn't want us to "*be unequally yoked together with unbelievers.*" Spending time with someone who doesn't believe in Jesus can pull you down and lead to heartache and despair.

Picture yourself pulling someone in a wagon up a hill. The larger the load and steeper the hill, the more strength it takes to pull that wagon. If the hill is at a slow incline but long, you will most likely run out of strength altogether. On the other hand, on the downhill slope you might have difficulty keeping control of that wagon. The steeper the hill, the tougher it will be to keep it from pulling you down. So it is with dating a non-believer. It's much easier for the unbeliever to pull you down than for you to pull him or her up. *1 Corinthians 15:33* clearly states:

Evil company corrupts good habits.

Are you keeping company with those who pull you down—away from the Lord? Ask God to give you the strength to walk away. He can replace them with people who can encourage you in your Christian walk.

_____

_____

_____

_____

_____

_____

_____

_____

_____

_____

See also *Ephesians 5:6-10;* and *1 John 1:5-7.*

Pride comes before a fall.

Read *Proverbs 16:18–19* and *1 Timothy 3:6*

There's a reason why God says in His word not to appoint a new believer to a position of leadership.[30] Tina began serving in areas of leadership within the first year she became born again. As a result, she became prideful and was judgmental of her brothers and sisters in Christ. Not long afterward she fell back into sin and was broken before God graciously drew her back into His ever-loving arms.

God resists the proud,
But gives grace to the humble.[31]

Has the Lord allowed you to serve in ministry? Do you ever compare yourself or think yourself better than, or of higher position, than others in the body of Christ?

_____

_____

_____

_____

_____

_____

_____

_____

_____

_____

_____

_____

_____

_____

_____

See also *Psalm 138:4-6; 2 Corinthians 7:10;* and *James 4:6*

There's nothing you do can to earn God's love. He proved His love on the cross.

Read *Romans 3:9-26* and *Ephesians 2:1-10*

Before the cross of Christ, the Jewish people did all they could to keep God's commandments. God knows that we all fall short; that not one of us can keep His commandments perfectly. That's why He sent His one and only Son to die. It is through faith in Jesus that we are made righteous in God's sight.

In Christ Jesus, God accepts you just as you are. You can't earn His love.

Are you trying to prove yourself worthy of God's love? List the Biblical truths about how, and why, you are loved by God.

See also Galatians 2:14-16; and *Titus 3:4-7.*

> You can still be disappointed in the church, even serving or working in ministry. The church and ministries are full of faulty, imperfect, emotional human beings.

Read *Matthew 18:1-35*

Tina knew better than to put her trust in people, including those in the church. Unfortunately that didn't keep her from being hurt. She's still human after all.

If you put the majority of your trust and faith in people rather than the Lord, you will always be let down and disappointed. On the other hand, if you keep your eyes on Jesus and make sure He's the reason you're serving in ministry and attending church services, you'll never be disappointed. He will give you the ability to see people through His eyes, and accept them for who they are and aren't.

Keep your eyes fixed on Jesus.

Have you been hurt by others? Are you looking to people for joy and fulfillment? Ask God to change your focus and give Him room to do so by spending time in prayer and reading His word, the Bible.

_____

_____

_____

_____

_____

_____

_____

_____

_____

_____

_____

_____

See also *Psalm 40:4-5; Psalm 62:8-9;* and *Micah 7:5-7.*

> **You can trust the Lord with your whole life; not just today, not just tomorrow, but every single day in every single way.**

Read *Matthew 6:25-34*

No matter what happens in life, God is on our side. He is in complete control and He cares about you more than any human ever could. He's the only one who sees the full picture and knows what's best for you. Put your trust in the One who knows all about you. He can give you peace.

God cares about you.
You need not worry about your life.

Does God care for the birds of the air and the lilies of the field? Does God value you more than the plants and animals He's created? He will take care of your needs. List that which causes you to worry and trust God with it all.

_____

_____

_____

_____

_____

_____

_____

_____

_____

_____

_____

_____

_____

See also *Proverbs 3:5-6; Philippians 4:6-7;* and *1 Peter 5:6-7.*

Are you living in two worlds; with one foot in the church and the other in the world? Living that way will leave you empty and broken. Return to One who loves you like no other; He is waiting for you.

Read *Luke 15:11-32*

The Lord delivered Tina from the snare of the evil one. He gave her Godly sorrow over the sin that caused her to run away from Him, and enabled her to fully repent. He will do the same for you. No matter how hard you try to run away from God, if you are His, He will bring you back so why wait?

Return to the God who doesn't give up on you.

Can you relate to the son who took his entire inheritance, left his father and wasted it all away only to be left eating among the pigs? Are you ready to return to your heavenly Father? He is waiting for your return and will welcome you with open arms.

_____

_____

_____

_____

_____

_____

_____

_____

_____

_____

_____

_____

_____

_____

See also *John 10:27-30; Romans 8:38-39;* and *Jude 1:24-25.*

God will continue weaving colors into your tapestry until you become the person He created you to be.

Read *Philippians 1:6* and *1 Thessalonians 5:23-24*

God finishes every project He starts. He has begun the process of weaving you into the person He created you to be. He's sanctifying you as you grow closer to Him each day you spend time with Him. He will be faithful to complete the tapestry of your life. You can trust Him.

God will complete the tapestry of your life.

Can you recognize the colors God has already woven into the tapestry of your life? Do you trust Him to complete the work He's begun in you or are you trying to weave the tapestry of your life without the Lord?

_____

_____

_____

_____

_____

_____

_____

_____

_____

_____

_____

_____

_____

_____

_____

See also *Ephesians 2:4-10; 1 Peter 5:10; Hebrews 12:2* and *Hebrews 15:20-21.*

Only God can wash the ugly stains of sin, and make you white as snow.

Read *Isaiah 1:18; 1 Peter 2:24-25;* **and** *1 John 5:11-13*

Christ died once, for all sinners, so that we might have life. Through the blood Jesus shed upon the cross, we can be washed clean.

Jesus died to give you life.

Have you accepted God's gift of salvation through the death and resurrection of Jesus? Have you allowed the blood of Jesus cleanse you from your sin?

_____

_____

_____

_____

_____

_____

_____

_____

_____

_____

_____

_____

_____

_____

_____

_____

_____

See also *Psalm 51:1-11; Micah 7:18-19; John 3:35-36; Hebrews 9:11-15;* and *1 John 1:7.*

God's love extends to all; He desires everyone to be saved.

Read *John 14:6* and *1 Timothy 2:3-6*

God's desire is for all to be saved: including me, including you. Tina was absolutely amazed at the extent of the love, mercy, and grace God has for her! She had only one way to respond. She turned away from her sin, put her faith and trust in Jesus, and started living her life for Him who so loved her.

There is only one way to the Father, by turning your life over to the One who died that you might live—Jesus.

So how can we keep this beautiful news to ourselves? Our desire should be to shout it from the rooftops!

Has God pulled you out of darkness and brought you into His everlasting light? Are you sharing the love and light of Christ with those around you?

_____

_____

_____

_____

_____

_____

_____

_____

_____

_____

_____

_____

See also *Luke 24:46-48; 2 Corinthians 5:14-15; 2 Peter 3:8-10; 1 John 4:9-10;* and *1 John 5:11-13.*

> # God so loved the <u>world</u> that He sent His only begotten Son to die so we might live.

Read *Romans 5:1–11; 8:31–39*

There's no reason whatsoever for God to love us. We're a rebellious, self-seeking, sinful people. So it makes no sense that God sent His own Son to die for humanity. The depth of God's love is absolutely incomprehensible. Regardless of whether or not we understand God's love, He loves us.

God loves you!

Most of us are familiar with the verse *John 3:16;*

> *For God so loved the world that He gave His only begotten Son, that whoever believes in Him should not perish but have everlasting life.*

But why? *Verse 17* tells us why:

> *For God did not send His Son into the world to condemn the world, but that the world through Him might be saved.*

Did you catch that? The creator of all heaven and earth loved the <u>world</u> so much that He sent His one and only Son to die so that **whoever** believes in Him won't die but will have everlasting life. God sent His Son that the <u>world</u> might be saved through Him.

I cannot begin to comprehend the depth of love God has for the <u>world</u>. I don't understand why He chose to reveal His love the way He did—by sacrificing His one and only Son for us. What I do know is that no man came up with the plan of salvation; it was God. Jesus is the only way to eternal life. Jesus is the truth and through Him is life.

See also *John 3:1–17, Romans 5:8;* and *Ephesians 2:4–9.*

God is strengthening you day by day that you might live in a way that brings Him glory.

Read *Romans 12:1-2* and *Ephesians 3:16-19*

As a caterpillar is transformed into a beautiful butterfly, so is God transforming you into something beautiful.

God renews and restores that which was once useless.

List some of the changes God has made in your life. Give God the praise and glory due His name for all that He is doing in your life.

_____

_____

_____

_____

_____

_____

_____

_____

_____

_____

_____

_____

_____

_____

_____

_____

_____

_____

_____

_____

_____

See also *2 Corinthians 5:17;* and *Philippians 1:9-11.*

You have been brought from death to life. Now that's a good reason for rejoicing!

Read *Psalm 138:1-8*

Praise God for what He's done for you. Rejoice and be glad! *Philippians 4:4* exhorts us to, *"Rejoice in the Lord always. Again I will say, rejoice!"*

Rejoice in the Lord!

What are some of the ways you can give God thanks, praise Him and rejoice?

_____

_____

_____

_____

_____

_____

_____

_____

_____

_____

_____

_____

_____

_____

_____

_____

_____

_____

See also *Psalm 5:11-12;* and *1 Thessalonians 5:16-18.*

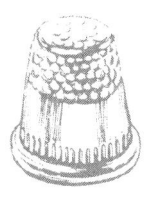

LESSON INDEX
Digging deeper

Dig a little deeper and allow the Lord to speak to your heart. More in-depth lessons are available for download at . . .
www.THREADSbyTeri.com

LESSON INDEX
(continued)

NOTES

1. www.rollinghillscovenant.com
2. www.lastwordsministry.com
3. www.romanandjorge.com
4. www.virtue.harvest.org
5. www.harvest.org
6. www.loganearthski.com
7. See *Hebrews 12:1-3*
8. www.seasidecommunitychurch.org
9. www.hopechapel.org
10. www.ccsouthbay.org
11. www.foapom.com
12. www.pageantofourlord.com
13. See *Luke 23:34*
14. www.gardentomb.com/about/brief-history
15. See *Mark 14:32-50*
16. See *Luke 22:43-44*
17. See *Matthew 4:18-22* and *Mark 1:14-20*
18. See *Matthew 5,6,7*
19. See *1 Samuel 16; Matthew 2:1-16; Luke 2:4-16; Micah 5:2*
20. See *1 & 2 Corinthians*
21. See *Ephesians*
22. See *Revelation 1:9*
23. www.loveinc.org, www.worldvision.org, www.worldvisionusprograms.org
24. www.*rose-publishing.com*
25. See *Hebrews 12:11*
26. www.celebraterecovery.com
27. See *Romans 3:23*
28. S. Michael Houdmann, *Got Questions Ministries*, 2002-2013 www.GotQuestions.org. Used by permission.
29. S. Michael Houdmann, *Got Questions Ministries*, 2002-2013 www.GotQuestions.org. Used by permission.
30. See *1 Timothy 3:6*
31. *James 4:6*

The names in this book have been changed out of respect for the privacy of the individuals mentioned.

TINA'S FAMILY TREE

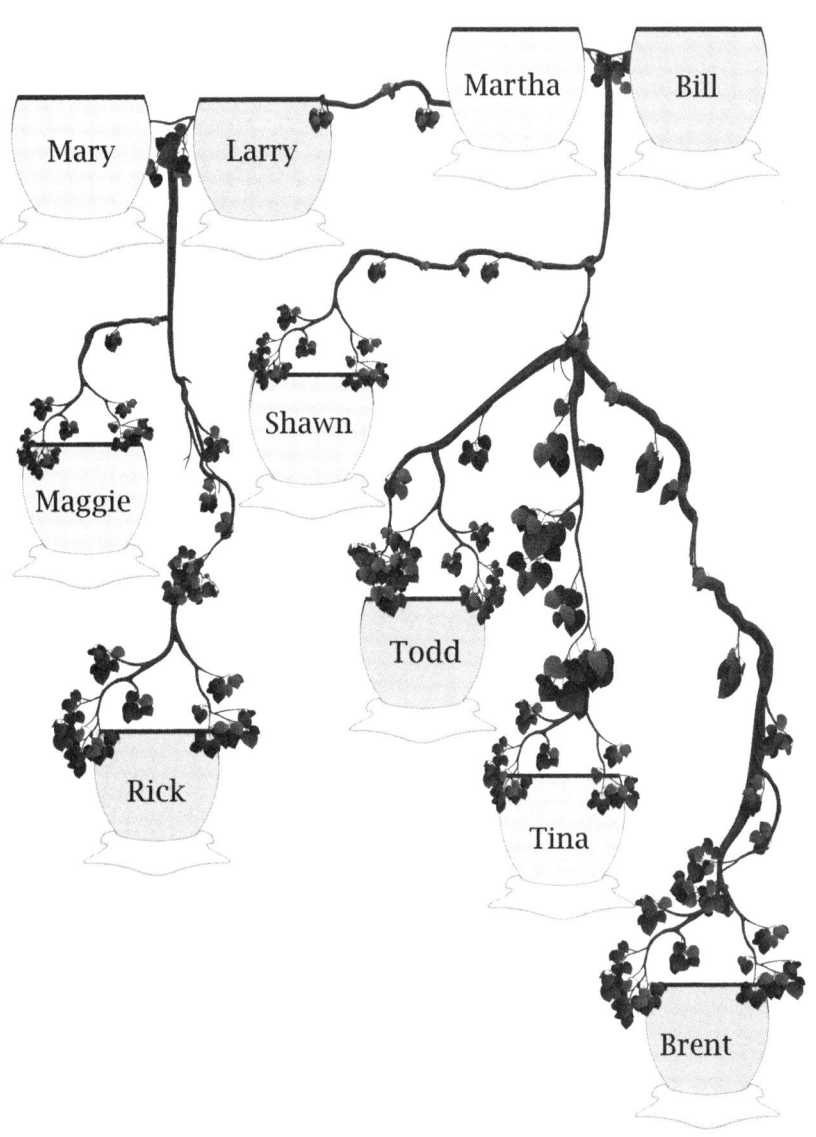

To God be all GLORY, HONOR, and PRAISE!

We can TRUST God. He is in CONTROL!

God COMFORTS
God TEACHES
God GUIDES
God PROTECTS

God LOVES

Download additional lessons at:
www.THREADSbyTeri.com

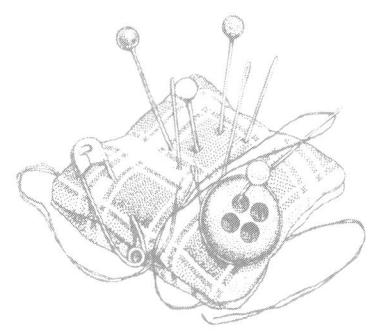